600—415

An Introduction to Modern Political Philosophy

Richer K. Li
Sunwakong@ yahou. com

An Introduction to Modern Political Philosophy

The Democratic Vision of Politics

Lesley A. Jacobs

Prentice Hall
Upper Saddle River, New Jersey 07458

Library of Congress Cataloging-in-Publication Data

Jacobs, Lesley A.
  An introduction to modern political philosophy : the democratic
vision of politics / Lesley A. Jacobs.
      p.   cm.
  Includes bibliographical references and index.
  ISBN 0-13-228826-5
  1. Political science—Philosophy.   I. Title.
JA71.J273   1997
320—dc20   96-27874
                                                              CIP

Acquisitions editor: Angie Stone
Editorial/production supervision: Marianne Hutchinson (Pine Tree
  Composition, Inc.)
Cover designer: Kiwi Design
Manufacturing buyer: Nick Sklitsis

This book was set in *10.5/12.5 Palatino* by Pine Tree Composition, Inc.,
and was printed and bound by *Courier Companies, Inc.*
The cover was printed by *Phoenix Color Corp.*

 © 1997 by Prentice-Hall, Inc.
Simon & Schuster/A Viacom Company
Upper Saddle River, New Jersey 07458

Printed in the United States of America
10   9   8   7   6   5   4   3   2   1

ISBN 0-13-228826-5

Prentice-Hall International (UK) Limited, *London*
Prentice-Hall of Australia Pty. Limited, *Sydney*
Prentice-Hall Canada Inc., *Toronto*
Prentice-Hall Hispanoamericana, S.A., *Mexico*
Prentice-Hall of India Private Limited, *New Delhi*
Prentice-Hall of Japan, Inc., *Tokyo*
Simon & Schuster Asia Pte. Ltd., *Singapore*
Editora Prentice-Hall do Brasil, Ltda., *Rio de Janeiro*

For Aaron, Grace, and Oliver

"The politician looks to the next election,
the statesman to the next generation,
and philosophy to the indefinite future."

(John Rawls, 1987)

Contents

Preface

------------------- ♦ -------------------

This book addresses three questions that are central to modern political philosophy: What is the nature of democratic government? Why are individuals morally bound to obey a democratic government? What is social justice in a democratic state? My treatment of these three questions serves as an introduction to some of the fundamental problems and issues in modern political philosophy.

   The central theme of this book is that it is impossible to answer any of these three questions separately. Instead, they must be addressed together as part of a comprehensive theory of democratic political morality. It is my intention, then, in this book to provide the reader with a brief sketch of a comprehensive theory of democratic political morality by examining the recent work of contemporary political philosophers. This broad theory I call *the democratic vision of politics.* The main idea is that the right to rule of a democratic government is conditional upon that right being exercised according to the requirements of social justice. Although it is possible to talk about the nature of democratic government without necessarily raising the issue of social justice, questions about individual rights to liberty, equality, and community must be addressed in order to explain the authority of the democratic state.

   This book has six principal chapters plus an introduction. The introduction is designed to situate our discussion of modern political philosophy within the broader framework of democratic theory. The first substantial part of the book is concerned with models of democratic government and theories of political obligation. Chapter Two surveys a number of models of democracy and ultimately defends the view that an ideal democratic state or democratic government is one that gives equal consideration to the interests of all citizens in its collective decision-making process. (For our purposes, the terms *democratic state* and *democratic government* can be used more or less interchangeably.) Chapter Three critically examines different theories about why an individual is morally bound to obey the laws of a democratic government.

The rest of the book is concerned with the role of social justice in the democratic vision of politics. The objective of Chapter Four is to explain the appeal of the language of rights to discussions of social justice in modern political philosophy. Chapter Five sets out to identify the place of individual liberty in a democratic state. This involves, on the one hand, a discussion of the complexities of the concept of individual liberty and why from a range of competing ideological perspective liberty is valuable and, on the other hand, an account of what it means for a government to take seriously rights to certain basic liberties.

The last two chapters of the book shift the focus to economic equality and community. Chapter Six argues that fundamental to the modern democratic vision is the idea that economic inequalities between citizens must be justified; such inequalities cannot be assumed to be "natural." Different political ideologies—liberal, conservative, libertarian, feminist, socialist, Marxist, postmodernist—disagree over how economic inequalities can be justified. While no particular ideology is favored, this framework is instructive because it brings clearly into the forefront the nature and scope of the disagreements among ideological factions within the modern democratic state. Chapter Seven concentrates on the recent revival of communitarian themes in modern political philosophy.

The motivation for writing this book comes from a general dissatisfaction with how students are often introduced to modern political philosophy. The tendency is to treat a range of ideas and concepts in a manner that does not demonstrate how these different ideas and concepts are related. My hope for this book is that the reader not only will gain some insight into what different contemporary political philosophers think about democracy, authority, rights, liberty, equality, community, and civil disobedience but also will acquire a sense of how these different ideas and concepts fit together into a coherent view of political morality. It is also important to realize that in this book, I am making philosophical arguments about political concepts. This means that I do not propose dictionary-like definitions but rather that I carefully present different views and subject them to criticism. Often, this criticism appeals to commonsense and shared intuitions; sometimes, it appeals to more philosophically sophisticated arguments. In general, though, it presupposes that readers have some rudimentary knowledge of day-to-day politics and the way in which their government is set up.

Although this book outlines and defends one particular interpretation of democratic political morality, the purpose is not to sway readers to that interpretation but instead to engage them so that they too can participate in the edifying conversation about political morality that is at present going on between modern political philosophers. I hope that by describing and criticizing other theories and ideas, this process will enable and encourage readers to criticize and argue against any views and eventually arrive at their own views about what are the fundamental features of the democratic vision of politics. The underlying point is that the best way to facilitate independence of thought among students seems to be to expose them to rigorous and careful arguments which reach controversial conclusions that encourage them to engage in philosophical debate.

It is important also to realize that this book is neither a comprehensive examination of democratic theory nor modern political philosophy. Democratic theory is far too rich and multifaceted to be comprehensively addressed in such a short book. (The brief introduction is designed to situate the treatment of modern political philosophy found in this book in the broader context of democratic theory.) Ideally, students should also be exposed to other sources in modern political philosophy. An excellent complementary text to this one is John Arthur and William Shaw, (eds.), *Social and Political Philosophy* (Prentice-Hall, 1992). That longer book contains many important essays written by a diverse group of eminent modern political philosophers. The value of the present book is that it puts the various views expressed in essays such as those into a broader perspective so that the reader is able to acquire an understanding of how those various views and ideas fit together.

Acknowledgments

$\blacklozenge$

Many people have helped me to write this book. By far, my greatest academic debt is to the undergraduate students at York University in Toronto and the University of British Columbia in Vancouver who heard much of this material in lecture format. Their insight and commonsense made an invaluable contribution to the presentation of the ideas I explore here. My own teachers shaped in a significant way the perspective on modern political philosophy that I defend here, in particular, G. A. Cohen, Ronald Dworkin, Geoffrey Marshall, T. R. Sansom, and Richard Vernon. I benefited greatly from research assistance by Willem Maas, Kimberley Montgomery, and Brian Nakata. I am also grateful to the following four reviewers for their helpful criticisms and suggestions: Bette Novit Evans (Creighton University), Gilbert S. Fell (Monmouth College), Franklin A. Kalinowski (St. Lawrence University), and Bruce Landesman (The University of Utah). Research funding was provided by a British Columbia Challenge Grant, the Faculty of Arts at York University, and the Social Sciences and Humanities Research Council of Canada.

My wife, Brenda, has been wonderfully supportive of my writing this book and others, often compromising her own career for the sake of mine. This book is dedicated to our three young children, Aaron, Grace and Oliver. Finishing this book has taken longer than I planned, partially no doubt because Aaron and Grace have been such a delightful distraction. Oliver arrived at the final stages of my completing this book and has been so cooperative and cheerful that, somewhat to my amazement, I have been able to meet my final deadline.

L.J.

Toronto

An Introduction
to Modern Political
Philosophy

CHAPTER ONE

Introduction

————————◆————————

"A great democratic revolution is taking place in our midst; everybody sees it, but by no means everybody judges it in the same way. Some think it a new thing and, supposing it an accident, hope that they can still check it; others think it irresistible, because it seems to them the most continuous, ancient, and permanent tendency known to history."
　　　　　—Alexis de Tocqueville, *Democracy in America* (1835)

§1　INTRODUCTION

The purpose of this book is to provide a sketch of the abstract political morality that lies at the foundations of modern democratic politics. The reason why we should take seriously the idea of a democratic political morality is obvious. Today, the citizens of modern industrial states are all democrats. Whatever disagreements they might have about the nature and function of their government, there seems to be a consensus around the view that their government must aspire to be democratic. The present age is, as Alexis de Tocqueville predicted more than 150 years ago, the age of democracy. But our thinking on the theory and practice of democracy has been multifaceted. This book focuses rather narrowly on abstract modern philosophical analysis of democracy. It neglects, therefore, many other important dimensions of democratic thought, not because these dimensions are insignificant or less fundamental but primarily because an examination of the disputes within modern political philosophy over democracy is in itself a daunting task. This chapter briefly explains what role modern political philosophy has in our understanding of democracy and how this role relates to questions about the history of the idea of democracy, the modern practice of democracy, and the background social conditions necessary for democracy. The general point is to situate our discussion of democratic political morality within the broader context of democratic theory.

§2   THE IMPORTANCE OF POLITICAL PHILOSOPHY

What is political philosophy? Why is it important? Why should anyone interested in understanding modern politics take it seriously? These are difficult questions, and, in fact, political philosophers disagree among themselves how to answer them. For the purposes of this book, I shall assume that political philosophy is concerned with questions about what I shall call political morality. *Political morality*, in this sense, raises issues about the ideal form of political rule and the scope and nature of what the government ought to do. The relevant contrast is to issues of *personal morality* where the central questions revolve around what I ought to do or what sort of character I should have. The focus on political morality can be either broad or narrow. When political philosophy has a broad scope, the emphasis is on developing, defending, and criticizing abstract general principles and ideals about, for example, the value of individual liberty and social equality with very little close attention to how those principles and ideals might be realized and worked out in practical situations and concrete instances. When the scope is more narrow, political philosophers might be concerned with discussing the values at stake in the debate over, for instance, the fairness of affirmative action programs or the censorship of pornography. This book tends to concentrate on the contributions of modern political philosophy to the more abstract principles of democracy; the concrete policy issues facing democratic governments are discussed primarily in order to illustrate broader, more general principles. The point is to sketch out broad abstract principles and ideals about what democracy is and what sort of policies it should aspire to. The use of the term "vision" is intended precisely to emphasize the general abstract characterization of democracy presented in this book.

    Having this vision is especially important for two reasons. The first reason is that these abstract philosophical principles provide us with a standard by which we can judge our current institutions. In other words, the abstract principles of democracy that are the focus of political philosophy enable us to make criticisms of existing political institutions and practices and to provide constructive suggestions for their reform or replacement. It is extraordinarily rare that a sustained political critique is not steeped in the language of political morality.

Perhaps the most striking recent example in our history is the civil rights movement. An important theme of that movement was the claim that America was not living up to its democratic ideal. The existence of racial discrimination, and especially its presence in political institutions, was said to be fundamentally incompatible with the democratic political morality that supposedly was at the foundation of American politics. (The classic statement of this critique is made by Gunnar Myrdal and his collaborators in the 1944 book *An American Dilemma: The Negro Problem and Modern Democracy*.) The power of this theme is evident throughout the 1950s and 1960s. Perhaps the most famous illustration is the speech by Martin Luther King, Jr., at the march on Washington on August 28, 1963. In that speech, King used the analogy of cashing a check to make his point:

> When the architects of our Republic wrote the magnificent words of the Constitution and the Declaration of Independence, they were signing a promissory note to which every American was to fall heir. . . . It is obvious today that America has defaulted on this promissory note insofar as her citizens of color are concerned. Instead of honoring this sacred obligation, America has given the Negro people a bad check, a check which has come back marked "insufficient funds." But we refuse to believe that the bank of justice is bankrupt. . . . So we've come to cash this check—a check that will give us upon demand the riches of freedom and the security of justice.

The point is that some knowledge of political philosophy is necessary to understand the motivation for the civil rights movement and its political significance.

The second reason for taking political philosophy seriously has to do with the very nature of democratic politics. Sometimes the conflict and disagreement that characterizes modern democratic politics is interpreted solely in terms of conflict of interest. The idea is that people disagree and conflicts arise because people in large industrial societies inevitably have conflicting interests. The political choices are said to be about choosing the means where the normative ends or objectives have already been settled. The difficulty with this interpretation is that sometimes it seems that there is more at stake. A vivid example is the polarized debate over abortion. It seems too simplistic to say that the disagreements between pro-life and pro-choice advocates have their source merely in a conflict of interests. A more defensible interpretation of the nature of democratic politics emphasizes not just disagreements about means but stresses that conflicts in politics are also over fundamental values and ends. (Berlin 1969: 118; 1980: ch. 5) The point is that often to understand certain issues and political strategies in the making of public policy, it is necessary to be sensitive to the more abstract, philosophical debates over fundamental values and ends. (See Kelman 1987.) In other words, the prospects for studying politics without recourse to moral values and principles are not promising. (Taylor 1985: ch. 2) This means, however, that political philosophy is fundamental to making sense of the politics of the modern democratic state.

§3   DEMOCRACY: THE HISTORICAL LEGACY

The idea of democracy has been taken seriously by political philosophers for more than 2,500 years. It was subject to criticisms by the ancient Greek philosophers Plato and Aristotle in the fourth century B.C. Democracy was revived by Machiavelli and other republicans and civic humanists in Italy in the fifteenth and sixteenth centuries. In England during the seventeenth century, John Lilburne and other so-called levelers demonstrated the radical potential of the idea of democracy and its link to social equality. Later that same century, John Locke developed a justification for revolution that invoked ideas ordinarily associated with democracy. In the eighteenth century, the revolutionary implications of the idea of democracy were sharpened by thinkers like Jean-Jacques Rousseau, Thomas Paine, and Thomas Jefferson. The American Revolution and the French Revolution illustrate vividly the political power of these ideas. By the late nineteenth century, under the influence of thinkers like James Mill, John Stuart Mill, and Alexis de Tocqueville, the ideal of democracy had come to have a central place in the political landscape. Twentieth century political theory and practice has been dominated by the goal of democracy.

For modern political philosophers, this historical legacy of democratic thought is immensely important and has had a profound influence on how we think about democracy today. However, this book will not emphasize this historical legacy nor illustrate its influence on modern political philosophy. Historically significant figures such as Locke or Marx are mentioned only in order to make points of contemporary relevance. This deliberate neglect of the historical legacy of democratic thought reflects the narrow focus of this book on modern political philosophy, and not a belief that this historical legacy is unimportant to understanding the theory and practice of democracy.

The fact that much of the literature on democratic political morality discussed in this book has been written in just the past thirty years demonstrates the incredible revival in political philosophy we have witnessed during this period. The single most important book written during this period is *A Theory of Justice* by the Harvard philosopher John Rawls, which was published in 1971. There were, however, numerous important contributions to political philosophy in the decade preceding the publication of Rawls's book, as well as countless valuable contributions since. Indeed, the surge of interest among philosophers in principles of political morality during the past twenty-five years has been so strong that it could be described as a modern renaissance in political philosophy. This book is designed to introduce the reader to the wide range of ideas on democracy and social justice in modern political philosophy.

§4 THE PRACTICE OF DEMOCRACY

Since this book does not have an historical orientation, the method of argument adopted follows that found in much modern Anglo-American analytic philosophy. The emphasis is on the coherence of the theories and concepts and on how well they stand up to (sometimes far-fetched) examples based on commonsense and intuition that challenge their central claims. As a result, the discussion is often quite abstract and says little explicitly about contemporary politics.

Nonetheless, it is significant not only that today most of us are committed democrats but also that those who live in the United States as well as most other western industrialized countries generally believe that their own governments are democratic. This fact means that modern political philosophers tend generally both to address the history of political thought and also implicitly to seek to advance and defend principles of democratic political morality that are consistent with their own governments appearing to be democratic. In other words, views about democratic political morality are constrained by contemporary practices of democratic institutions. Indeed, many contemporary democratic theorists begin by examining existing political institutions and gleaning from them their democratic features (if there are any).

This book is generally silent about the exact structure of the political institutions that characterize a democratic government, despite the large and excellent comparative politics literature on this subject. Obviously, this silence reflects partially a division of labor; a detailed study of institutions would detract from the central objective of providing a broad sketch of the democratic vision of politics. But this silence also reflects my belief that there is not a single answer to the question of what the institutions are that are demanded by the democratic vision of politics. The institutional differences between Britain's parliamentary system of government and the American republican system of federal government are stark, but it seems doubtful that one system can be praised as "genuine" democracy and the other dismissed as undemocratic simply because it is different. Nonetheless, commonsense suggests that there are certain institutional features shared by any system of government that aspires to be democratic. These features include a voting scheme which allows for participation by practically all citizens and involves elections at reasonably frequent intervals, some scope for majority rule, an adherence to the rule of law, and some measure of protection for individual rights and freedoms. Often, I shall draw on these familiar features to illustrate a point or support a criticism or make an argument.

Although modern political philosophy is constrained by existing political practices, it is important to realize that few political philosophers believe that our existing political system is perfectly democratic. As previously explained, political philosophy is important partially because it provides us with a standard against which we can criticize existing political institutions and practices. If modern political philosophers simply concluded that our existing institutions are democratic, then this fundamental critical function would dissolve.

However, it should be noted that some of the most interesting philosophical reflection on democracy has been generated in the context of explaining why certain existing institutions and practices that appear undemocratic are in fact consistent with democratic political morality. An excellent example is the long-standing debate in the United States over judicial review of legislation. (See, for example, Ely 1980; Dworkin 1985: ch. 2; Arthur 1995.) It is generally agreed that the Constitution forbids Congress and state legislatures from passing certain forms of legislation. The central problem is that there is no consensus on what forms of legislation are forbidden by the Constitution, because that document is often vague and ambiguous. Frequently, Congress or state legislatures pass legislation which is controversial because some people insist that it is forbidden by the Constitution. The institution of judicial review assigns to senior courts the task of reviewing such legislation and determining whether or not it is forbidden by the Constitution. Judicial review, therefore, means that a small elite group of unelected individuals have the power to overturn legislation passed by elected institutions reflecting majority rule and, in effect, have the power to make important political decisions. Isn't judicial review, then, at its base undemocratic?

How someone responds to this question necessarily presupposes an understanding of what democracy is. Among those who have defended judicial review on the grounds that it is consistent with and perhaps required by democratic principles, there have been a wide range of views about democratic political morality. Some have argued that the Constitution reflects the will (of the majority of) the people and that, provided courts interpret it literally, they are acting as mere agents of the people. The underlying belief here is that the essence of democracy lies in the idea of the will of the people. Others have argued that the essence of democracy is a commitment to political equality and that the forms of legislation forbidden by the Constitution reflect this commitment. So, provided that judicial review is carried out in a manner that maintains this commitment to political equality, then it is consistent with democratic principles. Regardless of one's own views on the relation between democracy and judicial review, there is no denying that the issue has promoted the use of democratic political morality as a tool for criticizing existing institutions and furthered our understanding of the philosophical issues at stake between competing abstract ideals of democracy.

§5 THE SOCIAL CONDITIONS FOR DEMOCRACY

Implicit in many discussions of democracy is the distinction between democratic government and democratic society. Democratic government refers specifically to the political institutions of a particular society. It is, however, frequently pointed out that the success of democratic governments depends on the existence of certain background social institutions such as a market economy and an independent television and newspaper media. Democratic society refers to those social institutions that are a prerequisite for democratic government. The point is that democracy is not just about political institutions but is also a matter of a particular form of civilization, sometimes called "democratic civilization." (Lipson 1964)

This book assumes that the context for questions about democratic political morality is large, industrial societies with a significant degree of ethnic and cultural diversity among its citizens. The core issues revolve around what it means to aspire to democratic politics in such societies and what are the normative foundations for the authority of a democratic government in that social setting. In other words, this book addresses the democratic vision of politics as it applies in Western Europe and North America.

However, in recent years, some of the most interesting theoretical work on democracy has focused on questions about the nature and structure of democratic society, that is to say, the background conditions necessary for successful democratic politics. This research has been spurred on by the recent political developments in Latin America, Eastern Europe, and the various republics that were once part of the U.S.S.R. These developments have reflected efforts to introduce more democratic governments. But these attempts at political reform have generated a barrage of questions about democratic society: What is the link between political democracy and economic reform? How important is so-called civil society to democratic politics? Are economic markets a prerequisite for democracy? Must market reforms be introduced by democratic governments? What place must the protection of private property have in a democratic system of government? Is democracy possible in a dual-ethnic society? Must the practice of religious toleration precede the introduction of democracy? What is the place of the military in the transition to democracy?

These sorts of questions are not especially new, although they have taken on a new urgency. However, for political philosophers in the past, perhaps the most important issue concerned the relation between social equality and democracy. The principal reason Tocqueville in 1835 in *Democracy in America* maintained that the coming age would be the age of democracy is that he saw a growing trend towards social equality and felt that democracy was inevitable in a society where a significant measure of equality exists. Since then it has often been argued that there is a fundamental tension between a hierarchical social class system and the existence of democratic government. (Marshall 1950) Likewise, as previously mentioned, one of the central themes in the civil rights movement of the 1950s and 1960s was that racial inequality is fundamentally incompatible with democracy. Indeed, fifty years ago, it was common to argue that the most pressing challenge in American politics was to reconcile the aspirations to democracy with the existing economic inequalities. (Becker 1941)

The importance of these sorts of critiques of social inequalities to political philosophy is worth emphasizing because they have encouraged modern political philosophers to examine carefully the concept of social justice. A central theme here is that it is difficult to make sense of current debates over social justice without situating them in the context of broader questions about democratic government. Most, if not all, major contributions assume, albeit not always explicitly, that the key issue is what social justice is in a democratic society. In fact, John Rawls, the author of the seminal book *A Theory of Justice*, maintains in his recent restatement and extended defense of the main arguments of that book that his theory of social justice must be understood as applying only to a democratic society and that many of the criticisms directed at his theory have not taken that context seriously. (Rawls 1993)

§6   CONCLUSION

This brief introduction has explained why studying modern political philosophy is important and how certain philosophical questions about democracy are related to other central questions about democracy. The purpose is to situate the abstract analysis of democratic political morality offered in the following chapters within the context of other central strands of democratic theory.

PART ONE

CHAPTER TWO

Models of Democracy

—————————◆—————————

§1   INTRODUCTION

Although today we are all democrats, there is little consensus about what exactly this means. Modern political philosophers disagree over what is the essence of democratic government. What distinguishes democratic governments from other forms of government? What is so special or unique about democracy? This chapter examines the different responses to these questions that can be found in modern political philosophy.

The idea of democratic government is an old one, dating back at least to Ancient Greece in the fifth century B.C. The term *democracy*, which is of Greek origin, can be literally translated as "rule of the *demos*, or people." That literal translation, though, does not specify what exactly "rule of the people" means. An elementary distinction can be made between direct democracy and indirect democracy. *Direct democracy* is any form of government in which all political decisions are made directly by the people who are subject to them. *Indirect democracy* is any form of government in which the people choose representatives to make political decisions on the people's behalf. For the most part, modern political philosophers have concentrated on the idea of indirect democracy, principally because direct democracy has not seemed a feasible alternative for large industrial societies.

Direct democracies do, however, exist. Perhaps the best known examples in the United States are the New England town meetings at which all members of small New England towns gather together to make decisions that affect their community. Certain Swiss cantons such as Geneva in the eighteenth century made political decisions in a similar fashion. Yet it has not seemed possible to translate the success of direct democracy in small communities into a form of government for large industrial societies of twenty-five million or more people. Moreover, it is the problem of how to rule these larger communities that has been the focus of modern political philosophy.

But this skepticism about the feasibility of direct democracy might appear misplaced, given the incredible advances in the development of information technology in the past couple of decades. This technological development makes it possible to imagine citizens of large industrial societies debating and voting on particular political issues in the comfort of their own home by way of their television or personal computer or touch tone telephone. (Wolff 1970: 34–37) However, this vision contains certain limitations. (Macpherson 1977: 95–98; McLean 1989: ch. 4) No matter how advanced the information technology is, it is still necessary to have someone or a group of people setting the issues that are to be debated and subject to voting; this situation suggests that some degree of indirect democracy is unavoidable.

This chapter focuses, then, principally on the idea of indirect democracy. For our purposes, it is possible to distinguish between two broad approaches to the idea of indirect democracy. Both approaches fixate on the fact that democratic government is a particular type of political procedure for making, implementing, and administering collective decisions that are binding on all citizens; but they differ with regard to what it is that makes particular collective decision-making procedures democratic. The first approach subscribes to what I shall call *convergent procedural democracy*. Here the main idea is that democratic governments are those that rule in the interests of the people, or *demos*, or what is often called the public interest or common good. The practical problem of democratic politics is to develop a decision-making procedure that makes collective decisions which serve the interests of the people. The second approach subscribes to what I shall call *fair procedural democracy*. According to this second approach, democratic government is characterized not so much by a concern to promote a particular outcome or goal, such as the interests of the people, but rather by a concern for making collective decisions in a manner that treats all citizens fairly. The essence of fair procedural democracy is the idea of political equality, not the public interest or common good.

Convergent procedural democracy and fair procedural democracy reflect very different ways of thinking about democratic government. These differences are not, however, unique to abstract philosophical discussions about the nature of democracy. They also underlie more concrete discussions of public institutions. Consider the case of courts administering criminal justice. There are two very different ways to look at courts in this regard. One way is to ask what is the ideal goal or outcome of the courts in their administration of criminal justice. The ideal outcome seems simple enough: find innocent people not guilty, and find guilty people guilty. The problem, then, for the administration of criminal justice by the courts is a practical one of designing trial procedures that promote this goal. Trials by a jury of one's peers and putting the onus of proof on the prosecution to establish guilt beyond a reasonable doubt are rules which might be defended because they appear to promote the ideal outcome of tracking innocence or guilt. Convergent procedural democracy reflects a very similar way of thinking about how collective decisions should be made by the government.

An alternative approach says that it does not make much sense to talk about the ideal outcome of the administration of criminal justice by the courts, since it is inevitable that the courts are not always going to achieve this outcome, no matter how perfect the rules or procedures might be. Instead, when we think about the courts, we should be concerned more fundamentally with whether their procedures are fair, and not whether they promote any particular outcome. Consider, for example, a rule like the so-called "right to silence" which says in effect that the refusal of a defendant to talk to law enforcement officers or to testify at his or her trial cannot be used as evidence for conviction. It is a standard observation that this rule serves the interests of the guilty and rarely promotes the ideal outcome of finding innocent people not guilty and guilty people guilty. However, the right to silence might simply be defended on the grounds of fairness, that is to say, on the grounds that it would be unfair to hold people's refusal to talk against them because of the fact that there are numerous reasons for such a refusal, not all of them suggesting guilt and worries about incriminating oneself. This alternative way of thinking about the courts administering criminal justice, with its emphasis on people being treated fairly, is very similar to how democratic decision-making is regarded by fair procedural democracy.

The tendency among democratic theorists has been, until very recently, to work within the framework of convergent procedural democracy. This chapter argues, however, that from a philosophical point of view, there are some serious problems with the main idea of convergent procedural democracy. I encourage the reader to embrace instead a particular version of fair procedural democracy.

§2.1   CONVERGENT PROCEDURAL DEMOCRACY

Convergent procedural democracy is characterized by the belief that the basic objective of democratic decision-making is to promote the interests of the people or what is more commonly referred to as the public interest or common good. Hence, within this approach, the basic problem for democratic theory is to find a form of government that produces decisions that converge with or promote a specific goal. Proponents of convergent procedural democracy disagree, however, over the general design of the collective decision-making procedure that will converge on the public interest or common good. For the sake of clarity, I will discuss these disagreements through an examination of four competing models of convergent procedural democracy. Models of democracy are abstract sketches of what are the essential features of democratic government. (Macpherson 1977; Held 1987) Often, models of democracy are oversimplified and too vague to give precise answers about the structure of democratic government. However, in philosophical discussions of democracy, competing models are useful because they allow us to focus on the main principles of political morality at issue within the convergent approach to procedural democracy. We shall critically examine in turn the four following competing models of convergent procedural democracy: the *classical* model, the *elite* model, the *market* model, and the *participatory* model.

Before turning to these models, it is necessary first to make some preliminary comments regarding the concept of the public interest or common good. (Although these two terms are sometimes differentiated, I shall treat them as more or less identical in meaning.) What do we mean by the public interest or common good? One possible answer is that the public interest or common good is simply a matter of those personal interests that all citizens in a state share in common. The virtue of this answer is that it presents a very clear and straightforward idea of the public interest or common good. The principal worry with this definition of the public interest or common good is that because in large industrial societies with a significant degree of cultural diversity, it is doubtful whether there are any personal interests that are shared by all citizens; this would mean, then, that there is no such thing as the public interest or common good in such societies. A second way to define the public interest or common good is by insisting that it is something distinct from the interests of specific citizens in a state. The public interest or common good, in this view, is in some sense abstracted from concrete individuals and instead reflects the shared communal belonging that is suggested by the very idea of a "demos;" the general point is captured by notions such as "community spirit" or the "public ethos" or "community standards." What worries many political philosophers about this definition is how it is possible for there to be any interest or good in a society which cannot be reduced, in the final analysis, to the interests or good of at least some of the citizens.

Alternatively, some say that the public interest or common good is what is in the best interests or the greatest good of the majority of citizens in a society. Underlying this third definition is a utilitarian ethic which requires that governments should act so as to maximize the greatest good (or happiness or utility or welfare) for the most people. The strength of this definition of the public interest or common good is that it associates those ideas with the personal interests of specific citizens but does so without restricting the relevant interests only to those shared by all citizens. In other words, this conception is operative in large industrial societies such as the United States. Furthermore, because this definition equates the public interest with the interest of the majority, it implicitly provides the normative foundations for why majority rule and other sorts of majoritarian standards should have a central place in democracy. Perhaps the most powerful objection to this definition is that it seems to make no room for the interests of minorities in the calculation of the public interest or common good.

The fourth way to define the public interest or the common good is to say that it is a matter of those interests that individuals have in common as members of the public. (Barry 1990: 190) The main point is that all citizens of a state share certain (public) interests by virtue of their shared citizenship, regardless of whether or not there is an overlap between their personal interests. Law and order and political stability are quintessential examples of shared interests in this sense. An important virtue of this understanding of the public interest or the common good is that it does not marginalize the interests of minorities. The most pressing difficulty with this fourth definition of the public interest or common good has to do with explaining why the interests we have as citizens matter other than because they serve our own personal interests. After all, if things like law and order matter only because they serve our own personal interests, it seems conceivable that in some cases, e.g., when you or I partake in criminal behavior, we may not in fact have an interest in law and order.

These last two definitions of the public interest or common good have held the most sway for modern political philosophers. As we shall see, they both have a basic role in the various models of convergent procedural democracy. But it is very important to realize that what is at stake among these four different competing models is often not how to define the public interest or the common good but rather how to design procedures for democratic collective decision-making that converge on the public interest or common good, however it is defined. This is because a particular definition of the public interest or common good does not always answer what is, in a specific instance or context, the public interest or common good. And indeed, under the convergent approach to procedural democracy, a fundamental feature of democratic politics is deciding what in a specific instance is the public interest or common good.

§2.2   THE CLASSICAL MODEL

The *classical* model of convergent procedural democracy holds that the best procedure for making political decisions that serve the common good is to have the people or electorate vote for individual candidates in an election and for the successful candidates to assemble and carry out the will of the people. (Schumpeter 1950: 250) The assumption that underlies this model of democracy is that the people know what is in the common good or public interest. Nevertheless, because of the practical problems with direct democracy previously mentioned, it is not possible for the people to make political decisions directly. It is, therefore, necessary for the people to elect officials who can carry out the will of the people. And by doing so, those elected officials will serve the common good.

The nature of the classical model of democracy can be clarified through a brief consideration of the different ways in which an elected official might represent those people who elected her or him. One way is for the elected official to act simply as a delegate for the people, that is, she or he will simply convey the views of her or his constituents to a general assembly or legislature. Another quite different way is for an elected official to act independently of the particular views of his or her constituents but nevertheless in what the official perceives to be the interests of his or her constituents. To illustrate, imagine that you are a member of a political party and that you have been chosen to represent your local district at a party leadership convention. Whom should you support in the leadership race? If you are simply a delegate for the people of your local district, then you should support whoever is the preferred candidate in your district. On the other hand, if you are thought to have more independence, then you should support whoever you think would be the best candidate, regardless of what the people in your own district might think. The relevant point is that on the classical model, elected representatives in a democracy are to be delegates of the people and not to have the sort of independence that allows them to make their own judgments about what is in the common good.

The virtues of the classical model of democracy are undeniable. It is very much in the spirit of Abraham Lincoln's famous call in his Gettysburg speech of 1863 for "government of the people, by the people, for the people." While correcting for the problems of direct democracy, it ultimately leaves the power to make political decisions in the hands of the people, since the elected officials will only be carrying out the will of the people. This fact, then, clearly distinguishes democracy from forms of government like aristocracy, which are commonly understood to be rule by the few, not the many. Moreover, the classical model offers a clear explanation of how a decision-making procedure can be designed so that the outcomes of that procedure converge on a desirable goal, that is to say, the public interest or common good.

But, despite these virtues, the classical model of democracy has at least four serious flaws. The combination of these four flaws makes it difficult to entertain the classical model as a serious option for democratic governments. The first problem concerns the assumption that the people really do know what is in the public interest or common good, complicated by the difficulty of defining what exactly *is* the public interest or common good. But the optimism about the people knowing the public interest, whatever it is, is built on the belief that there is a well-educated public who are genuinely interested in knowing what is in the common good. In fact, though, this belief seems a very dubious one; most ordinary people are concerned for the most part with their own self-interest and the interests of those around them. This is not to say that people are inherently selfish, just that most people have a limited capacity to entertain the broad sort of concern that is implicit in the very idea of the common good.

The second questionable feature of the classical model follows on the point just made. The classical model envisions the electorate bringing to its elected officials a view of what is in the common good that it is then the job of the elected official to carry out. However, there is, according to many critics, a sense in which this model of democracy has gotten the process backwards. It is not so much that the electorate has a view which elected officials carry out but rather that, ideally, candidates for election offer the electorate different views of what is in the common good, and then the electorate endorse the view of whomever they elect. It is in this sense that we commonly speak of an elected official or party having a mandate to carry out their election platform. The difficulty, then, with saying that the people know what is in the public interest or common good and that the role of elected officials is to carry out the will of the people, is that in all likelihood it is the elected officials who have had the primary role in shaping the people's view of what is presumably in the public interest. The following experience of a businessman who sent two salesmen to Africa after the Second World War to explore the possibility of expanding his shoe sales there will illustrate my basic point. One salesman sent back a telegram saying that because nobody wore shoes in Africa, there was no market to develop in Africa. The second salesman wired an enthusiastic telegram saying that he thought that the potential market in Africa was terrific; after all, since no one seemed to have shoes, all the firm had to do was to convince people that they needed shoes.

The third flaw with the classical model of democracy is a reflection of a more general problem with the very notion of conceiving elected officials as delegates of the people. The difficulty here is that this presupposes a consensus among the people whom the official represents, but rarely is there consensus of this type among the electorate. In most cases, the electorate hold a diverse range of views which it is unlikely or impossible for any single elected official to act on in a coherent fashion. Ultimately, when the views of some of the official's constituents conflict with the views of some of the other constituents, it is necessary for the elected official to make a judgment about whose views to represent, with the result that he or she cannot be a delegate for the views of some of the constituents.

The fourth flaw is independent of the first three. So far, I have expressed skepticism about the capacity of the people to know genuinely what is in the common good. Let us suppose, however, that this skepticism is misplaced and that the people do genuinely have this knowledge. The soundness of the classical model also depends on the further claim that the people will act on the common good. Yet this claim is also a dubious one. All too often policies that are widely believed to serve the public interest or common good are immensely unpopular. Taking measures to increase taxation in order to reduce the government's spending deficit is a standard example. The simple point is that in politics, knowing that some law or policy will serve the public interest or common good does not always seem to motivate public officials to support such laws or policies.

§2.3   THE ELITE MODEL

We have just seen that the classical model of democracy is objectionable in at least four respects. It is important, however, to realize that these criticisms do not defeat the very idea of convergent procedural democracy. A central theme in modern political philosophy has been to develop alternative models of convergent procedural democracy that do not suffer from the same faults that characterize the classical model. One such alternative is the *elite* model of democracy.

The elite model of democracy assigns to the people or electorate the primary role in choosing representatives to make political decisions with the objective of promoting the public interest or common good. But this model, unlike the classical model, does not regard these representatives as mere delegates of the people, who act on the people's view of what is in the common good; instead, because these representatives have their own ideas of what is in the public interest, their role is to make political decisions that reflect those ideas. The fundamental point is that it is this small, select group of individuals who make political decisions under this model of democracy. The people are important only insofar as they determine the makeup of this elite group during periodically held elections.

One of the principal strengths of the elite model of indirect democracy is that the parliamentary system of government that exists in Canada, Great Britain, and a number of Western European countries conform to it. The politics of these countries are dominated by competitive political parties, each seeking support from the electorate during elections held every four or five years. Whichever party wins the election forms the government and assumes control over the political decision-making process. There is a consensus that politics of this sort is democratic; the elite model of democracy explains why this is the case (Schumpeter 1950: 273–283).

The elite model of democracy is superior to the classical model in a number of very important respects. The most striking, given the criticisms of the classical model discussed before, is that the elite model does not depend on the people knowing what is in the public interest or common good. The elite model shifts that burden to the small group of elected individuals who have the task of governing. This seems to be a more reasonable stance, since it does seem plausible to think that at least some people will know what is in the common good, even though the vast majority will lack the requisite political imagination. Another significant feature of the elite model is that it is able to explain how a democratic government can introduce a measure that is immensely unpopular; the explanation is that because the elite know what is in the public interest, they are introducing a measure to serve that objective, but because the vast majority of the people do not fully grasp what is in the common good, they therefore do not see why such a measure is needed. (This sort of reasoning often underlies the introduction of unpopular tax measures.)

The most obvious problem with the elite model of democracy is that it is not altogether clear why what it recommends should be construed as a form of democratic government in the first place. Would it not be more appropriate to describe it, as Rousseau does, as an "elective Aristocracy" since it involves rule by the few? (Rousseau 1762: 59) *Democracy* literally means, as stated earlier in the chapter, "rule by the demos, or people." But it is not at all apparent in what sense the people rule under the elite model; at most, the people choose their rulers, but the pertinent question is whether this process can really be construed as ruling.

Even if we put this problem aside, the elite model of democracy can also be criticized insofar as it puts much faith in the elected leaders to serve the common good, provided that they know what the common good is. If there are good reasons to be suspicious of the proposition that the people know what is in the common good and seek policies that will serve that end, it seems that there are even stronger reasons to be suspicious of a political procedure which relies on an elite leadership to act in the common good; the scope for corruption is overwhelming. The standard response to this worry is that elections will keep the leadership accountable. However, this response presupposes that the people know what the common good is and can thus identify when the elected leadership has strayed from it; the problem, in other words, is that this response makes sense on the classical model of democracy but not on the elite model, since it is the classical model that is built on the assumption that the people know what is in the common good. The elite model arises out of a deeply felt skepticism about that assumption.

§2.4   THE MARKET MODEL

The objection that the *elite* model of democracy may not be a genuine model of democracy because it seems to make little room for the people to rule suggests a general problem for any type of indirect democracy in which the people do not participate directly in the everyday political decision-making process but instead choose representatives to do it for them. The general problem is that under any model of indirect democracy, it seems inevitable that there will be a certain degree of sacrifice of the principle that the people should rule; the issue is just how much sacrifice is consistent with the basic idea of democracy. (Dahl 1989: 30) Because the *elite* model excludes the people from any input into the decision-making procedure other than through elections, it is a dubious model of democracy. Although the *classical* model assigns to the people a major role in the decision-making procedure, this assignment rests on the problematic assumption that the people know what is in the common good.

The *market* model of convergent procedural democracy offers a more compelling response to the issue of how the people can be involved in the decision-making procedure and yet yield policies that serve the public interest or common good than does either the *classical* model or the *elite* model. The *market* model accepts the idea that it is unlikely that people do genuinely know what is in the common good and that even if they do know, it is not necessarily the case that they will act on that knowledge instead of on some other perceived good. Nevertheless, unlike the *elite* model, the *market* model still accepts that the people should be actively involved in the democratic procedure of decision-making. The main idea is that democratic politics should be a competition between individuals and groups, with each pursuing its own self-interest without regard for the interests of other people competing in the same process. The market model of democracy maintains that by having individuals and groups within society all pursuing their own interests within the political decision-making process, the unintended consequence will be that the public interest or common good is served.

The central insight that this model of democracy brings to bear on its analysis of political decision-making procedures is the idea that political procedures can operate in a fashion very similar to the way that markets for goods work in the economy. Classical economic theory of markets analyzes the collective action involved in allocating and distributing resources in a nation's economy in terms of individual behavior and choices. The assumption made is that in economic exchanges between individuals, the choices and behavior of each individual do not reflect a concern with what is good for the other individual but rather reflect his or her pursuing what he or she perceives to be good or desirable, whether that is his or her own self-interest or something else. The idea, then, is that if I go into a shop to buy some cheese, I seek to pay a price for the cheese that reflects, for example, my own self-interest and not what is in the interest of the shopkeeper; in other words, I will try to pay as little for the cheese as I reasonably can. An economy that uses markets to allocate resources is based on these kinds of economic exchanges between individuals. Classical economic theory holds that the market, through what Adam Smith famously described as the "invisible hand," coordinates these economic exchanges so that their net result is an economy that serves the common good. Thus, the point is that the common good is served even though no single individual aims to serve that end.

The innovative feature of the market model of convergent procedural democracy is, then, precisely that it says that a political decision-making procedure modeled on economic markets will be an effective process for converging on the outcome of serving the common good. There is, on this model, nothing objectionable about citizens and their elected representatives seeking their own self-interests through the political process. Indeed, the electoral system *should* be designed to facilitate this sort of pursuit of self-interest, since, as with economic exchanges, the objective of serving the common good would be frustrated if individuals sought to realize that objective in their own choices and behavior. (This factor distinguishes it from *explanatory* empirical analysis of actual political institutions that emphasize the behavior of political agents such as political parties can be predicted by making the assumption that they are self-interested, utility-maximizing agents. (See, for example, Downs 1957.) What the classical and elite models of democracy perceive as dangerous to democratic decision-making, the market model identifies as the essential requirement of any collective decision-making procedure that is designed to converge on the public interest or common good.

Although the market model is an extraordinarily cogent version of convergent procedural democracy, it can, nonetheless, be criticized at a very fundamental level. The strength of the model rests on the analogy to the case made by classical economic theory for a market-based economy. It is extremely important to notice, however, that this case for economic markets is, in effect, a utilitarian one; that is to say, economists like Adam Smith maintain that a market economy will produce the greatest utility for the most people. This means, though, that the market model rests on the claim that the marketlike political process which it recommends will maximize the interests of the most people; this does not mean either that it will treat everyone fairly or that everyone will have some of her or his interests served by it. (Likewise, classical economic theory does not claim either that everyone—for example, the physically or mentally disabled—will be treated fairly by a market economy or that everyone will benefit to some degree from it.)

The fact that the market model would not necessarily treat all citizens fairly seems at odds with the very idea of democracy. Let me illustrate this tension with a particular issue of contention among proponents of the market model. Some of them contend that taking the economic market analogy seriously in a democratic process means allowing for the buying, selling, and trading of votes in a legislative assembly, as well as in elections to that assembly. (Buchanan & Tullock 1962: ch. 9) Most people, however, find this proposal disturbing; votes in a democracy should not be up for sale. The reason seems to be that this situation would be unfair because the result would be that the wealthy who could afford to buy extra votes would have much more political influence than the poor. (Barry 1990: chs. 14–15) But this suggests generally that it is not enough for defenders of the market model of democracy to show that political decision-making procedures that are modeled on economic markets serve the interests of the greatest number in society; they must also show that these marketlike political procedures are in fact fair.

Of course, a major theme of recent work on distributive justice by political philosophers and economists has been the issue of when market-based outcomes are fair. (Varian 1975; Dworkin 1981; Jacobs 1993b) This work has emphasized that it is inevitable that sometimes the requirements of fairness are going to require a decision that does not maximize the good of the greatest number. This situation means, then, that priority must be given either to being fair or to maximize utility or goodness. The market model of convergent procedural democracy gives priority to maximizing the utility of the greatest number, but this fact leaves it open to the objection that it results in not everyone's being treated fairly. We shall see later in this chapter that models of fair procedural democracy are an improvement on the market model precisely because, although they too emphasize the idea of the democratic process as a forum for the competing interests of individuals and groups, they are not open to this objection.

§2.5   THE PARTICIPATORY MODEL

We have just seen that a model of convergent procedural democracy which presupposes that individual citizens pursue their own self-interest is problematic. Earlier, we found that models requiring the people or an elite group of representatives to know what is in the common good and act on that knowledge are also problematic. Is there an alternative model of convergent procedural democracy?

Recently, there has been a revival of the idea of participatory democracy. Often participatory democracy is confused with direct democracy. Recall that direct democracy is best understood through a contrast to indirect democracy. Whereas direct democracy is a form of government in which all political decisions are made directly by the people who are subject to them, indirect democracy is any form of government in which the people choose representatives to make political decisions on their behalf. Direct democracy is not feasible in large industrial societies. The issue for the *participatory* model of democracy is how indirect democracy can be designed to facilitate for more participation by ordinary citizens.

The point that is seized upon by the *participatory* model is the fact that criticisms of the *classical* model of convergent procedural democracy take the people or electorate as they presently are. Who can deny that at present the electorate in most Western liberal democratic countries lack a coherent vision of the common good and emphasize instead their own myopic self-interest? Yet the participatory model says that this condition is a consequence of our present political system, not an unchangeable and natural feature of the electorate. What must be realized is that it is a social and political achievement for a people to have a vision of the common good. This is an achievement that is nurtured and developed, not something an electorate either has or doesn't have. How can an electorate be transformed so that it has a coherent vision of the good? The response inherent in the participatory model is through participation in the making of collective decisions. (Barber 1984: ch. 6) To put the point a bit strongly, participation in political institutions is a sort of civics lesson that educates the people about what is the common good and why they should promote it.

A very simple (and idealistic) version of participatory democracy is one that organizes the decision-making procedure in the form of a pyramid. (Macpherson 1977: 108–112) At the base of the pyramid is a significant degree of direct democracy in local forms of community, such as local neighborhood groups, factory worker associations, etc. These forms of community would discuss issues and make decisions, perhaps based on some sort of majority rule. They would then elect delegates to take their concerns to a slightly higher level of the pyramid, such as city or district councils. Delegates at this level would remain directly accountable to the more basic forms of community at the base of the pyramid. These councils would in turn choose delegates for associations at higher levels on the pyramid, such as, for example, county or state governments. And so on until the top of the pyramid is reached. Practical variations on this ideal tend to emphasize the importance of local governments as the sites for the making of public policy and collective decisions.

The participatory model of convergent procedural democracy has a certain intuitive appeal which is undeniable. It also has a long history dating back at least to Thomas Jefferson, who, in response to certain critics of democracy, commented, "If we think [the people] not enlightened enough to exercise their control with a wholesome discretion, the remedy is not to take it from them, but to inform their discretion." Moreover, unlike the classical model, the participatory model does not presuppose an especially optimistic view of the people as they are; all it requires is that it be possible for them to change and be transformed in the future.

There are two related principal problems with the participatory model of convergent procedural democracy. The first problem has to do with how political participation is conceived of in that model and, therefore, who participates. Feminists have emphasized that in practice participatory models have been dismal at promoting political participation by women. (Pateman 1989: ch. 9; Phillips 1991: ch. 5; Mansbridge 1986: chs. 1, 2, 13) An explanation is that participatory approaches to democracy do not typically challenge, but rather presuppose, a public/private distinction that has traditionally excluded women from political action. The important roles women have assumed are relegated to the private sphere, leaving them with far fewer opportunities than men to assume a role in the public sphere. For example, the family demands of caring for young children are regarded as a matter for the private sphere and are a burden carried overwhelmingly by women; those demands, though, seriously curtail a person's ability to participate in politics. (The observation that political activism takes far too many evenings is especially insightful in explaining why in public affairs mothers with young children are notably absent.)

The other related problem with the participatory model has to do with what it expects from individual citizens. Modern industrialized societies are characterized by what can be described as the fact of pluralism. (Rawls 1987: 4) This is the fact that individuals in our society pursue a wide range of life-plans. These life-plans are very diverse and frequently conflict. Often, these life-plans make no room for any sort of sustained participation in political institutions and collective decision-making. The truth is that many people in our society have no interest in political participation; this is not so just because presently our political institutions do not encourage it but also because people just do not regard it as an important priority in their lives. Can these people be compelled to participate in democratic decision-making? The participatory model emphasizes the voluntary dimension of participation; people can refuse to participate if they so choose. But this raises serious questions about who is getting educated about the common good and whether this genuinely is the common good. After all, since it seems likely that many people in large industrial societies will choose not to participate, one is left wondering who it is that is getting involved and how much of a reflection the person is of the people or electorate in general. In a sense, the participatory model will seem to lead to some sort of self-selected elite who are making collective decisions and representing those decisions as promoting the common good. However, we then have good reason to be as skeptical about this model as about the elite model of convergent procedural democracy.

§3.1   FAIR PROCEDURAL DEMOCRACY

So far, we have examined four different models of convergent procedural democracy and found each wanting in certain very important respects. Although these four models do not exhaust the logically possible variations on convergent procedural democracy, the criticisms that I have leveled at them raise serious doubts about the cogency of *any* model of convergent procedural democracy. For this reason, we shall turn our focus to the idea of fair procedural democracy. The distinctive feature of democratic government, according to this approach, is political equality.

Fair procedural democracy has provided the context for, in my view, the most important and innovative recent work in democratic theory. (Dahl 1989; Beitz 1989; Przeworski 1991; Jones 1983) As we saw at the outset of this chapter, the idea of fair procedural democracy does not identify democratic decision-making procedures with any particular outcome. Thus, the problem of democratic government with this approach is not to design a decision-making procedure that converges on some desired outcome like the public interest or the common good. Instead, the problem for fair procedural democracy is to design a political decision-making procedure that treats all members of the state fairly in the process of making, implementing, and administering public policy. What distinguishes democratic government from other forms of government like aristocracy or monarchy is that the concern lies with treating all members of the state fairly, not just a small minority.

When is a political decision-making procedure fair? For our purposes, it is useful to start by distinguishing between *procedural fairness* and *background fairness*. (Barry 1990: 97–99) Procedural fairness occurs when a certain set of rules are followed. Consider a boxing match. The outcome of the match is procedurally fair provided that the fight did not involve the violation of any rules, such as punching after the bell has gone off. The point is that the winner of the match is whoever scores the most points or knocks out the opponent, provided that certain agreed-upon rules of conduct are met. Background fairness is a matter not of compliance to certain rules of conduct but rather of the notion that those involved in the procedure are in some sense fairly matched. In the case of boxing, for example, background fairness requires that boxers be in the same body weight category. It would be a violation of background fairness to have a fight between a welterweight boxer and a heavyweight boxer.

Procedural fairness and background fairness are both important to fair procedural democracy. While I shall concentrate on procedural fairness, it is important to see also the relevance of background fairness. Background fairness arises in the case of everyday political issues like the funding of political campaigns for public offices. It would seem to be contrary to background fairness for one candidate to have much greater financial resources than another candidate; in a sense, they would not be fairly matched. For this reason, it makes sense to have some sort of public financing of political campaigns. Another tricky issue of background fairness arises in the United States where incumbent politicians appear to have a much better chance of winning elections than do other candidates. In the New York senate, for example, incumbent senators running for reelection have a success rate above 95 percent. This situation puts challengers at a distinct disadvantage; yet, background fairness requires that this disadvantage be addressed. The difficulty is finding a policy solution that addresses this problem.

Let us, however, put aside background fairness and concentrate on procedural fairness. What are the rules that make a democratic political decision-making procedure fair? Consider again that *democracy* in Greek means literally "rule by the *demos*." Fair procedural democracy fixates on the fact that the demos is "a citizen body consisting of members who are considered equals for purposes of arriving at governmental decisions." (Dahl 1989: 83) Thus, for a political decision-making procedure to treat all citizens fairly, it must treat them as equals. In other words, fair procedural democracy is a system of government that treats all of its citizens as equals. The essence of democratic government is political equality.

When does a collective decision-making procedure treat its citizens as equals? Proponents of fair procedural democracy say that a procedure treats everyone as equals when it gives equal consideration to the interests of everyone involved; not to do so is tantamount to not treating everyone as an equal. Competing models of fair procedural democracy differ over what exactly is involved in a collective decision-making procedure that gives equal consideration to the interests of all citizens. While convergent procedural democracy has given rise to numerous different models of democracy, discussions of fair procedural democracy have mainly been limited to two basic models, the *neutrality* model and the *egalitarian* model of fair procedural democracy. The following discussion explains how these two models can be distinguished and why the egalitarian model is more defensible.

§3.2   THE NEUTRALITY MODEL

The *neutrality* model focuses on the question, Who is the best judge of a citizen's interests? The reason why this question is such a poignant one is that it puts a finger on the basic assumption of much modern democratic theory that individuals are generally the best judges of what is in their own best interests. (Dahl 1989: 99) This assumption says, in other words, that when there is disagreement about what is in your best interest, your view, not the government's or anyone else's, should prevail. This assumption has forceful political implications because it rules out the possibility that a government not of our own making can serve our interests better than a democratic government.

The neutrality model of fair procedural democracy seizes upon the fact that the view that individuals are generally the best judges of what is in their own best interests also has significant implications for the idea that the interests of all citizens be given equal consideration in a democratic political process. It suggests that what a decision-making procedure must do is take into consideration the interests of each citizen according to what each citizen judges to be his or her own interests. Moreover, to do this in a fair manner requires that those interests be given equal weight in the determination of any particular decision. Political decision-making is, then, a matter of weighing up all these (frequently conflicting) interests and reaching a conclusion that reflects a compromise between them.

The attractiveness of this model of fair procedural democracy is that it emphasizes the importance of the participation of each individual citizen in the decision-making process. This participation is essential because each citizen knows what is in his or her best interests. Although elected officials may be important for designing policies that serve those interests, but they do not have the role of judging what those interests are. This power remains in the hands of the *demos*. (It is similar in this respect to the market model of convergent procedural democracy.)

Unfortunately, though, the strength of the neutrality model is also its weakness. What would characterize the politics of a government that aspired to the neutrality model of fair procedural democracy? Perhaps the most striking image is that of individual citizens each making claims on the political process regarding what is in their particular interests. The difficulty is adjudicating among these claims. How do we decide which claims are valid and which are illegitimate? The neutrality model starts from the assumption that each citizen is the best judge of what is in his or her interest. This means, though, that neither public officials nor the political process in general can evaluate the merits of the various claims that citizens present about what is in their interests. A democratic government must be "neutral" between these interests. (Ackerman 1980; Dahl 1989: 87) It follows that all claims about a citizen's interests must be taken at face value.

But this neutrality has unsavory consequences, for democratic decisions that follow this procedure end up being merely bargained outcomes between the various claims of different citizens. The outcomes simply reflect the diverse character of the claims that constitute the inputs into the process. Reducing democratic decision-making to a bargaining process can be shown to be problematic in at least two important respects. The first problem concerns the issue of whose claims are heard. When democratic politics revolve around a process of claims-making, it seems inevitable that those people who, for example, have more economic clout will be better able to ensure that their claims are heard. It is doubtful that this condition meets either procedural fairness or background fairness. Yet, the neutrality model lacks the moral resources to preclude this from happening. The second problem concerns how certain issues will be resolved in a democracy that aspires to neutrality. Consider, for example, the legal issue of criminal prohibitions against homosexual acts. In the past thirty years, most (but certainly not all) states have removed these sorts of prohibitions and other types of antisodomy legislation from their legal codes. This trend has also occurred in Western Europe. In most instances, the case against antisodomy laws is generally presented as an issue of equality. Antisodomy laws are typically said not to treat homosexuals as equals. These laws are typically defended on the grounds that homosexual acts are debased and contrary to a community's moral standards of decency and that a majority of citizens support their existence. Under the neutrality model, whether or not there should be antisodomy laws is fundamentally to be decided by what most people would prefer. (Bork 1990: ch. 7) But this neglects the fact that in this case what some people prefer is that the law treat other people as less than equals. (Hart 1983: 213–221; Dworkin, 1985: 365–372) It seems absurd that a political decision-making procedure committed to political equality would take such preferences seriously. Yet, the neutrality model of fair procedural democracy, because of its professed foundational commitment to being neutral towards the interests of different citizens, is hard pressed to explain why not. Moreover, it is significant that the example of antisodomy laws is not unique; the neutrality model would also be hard pressed to dismiss racist or sexist views.

§3.3   THE EGALITARIAN MODEL

Fair procedural democracy requires, as mentioned previously, that the interests of all citizens be given equal consideration in the decision-making process. Different models offer competing interpretations of what this abstract requirement entails. We have just seen that the neutrality model fails because it is unable to distinguish among the citizens' interests those which are worthy of consideration from those which are not. This failure has important implications insofar as it allows for the possibility that a democratic government would have to take seriously the preferences of some citizens that other citizens be treated as less than equal. This implication seems so counterintuitive to the very idea of fair procedural democracy that it makes the neutrality model untenable. It has encouraged some prominent political philosophers such as Ronald Dworkin to shift their sympathies from the neutrality model to the *egalitarian* model of fair procedural democracy. (Dworkin 1983)

From the perspective of the egalitarian model, what the neutrality model loses sight of is the fact that fair procedural democracy aspires to a collective decision-making procedure that treats all citizens as equals. The commitment to giving equal consideration to the interests of all citizens flows from this more general aspiration. This means, though, that a procedure giving equal consideration to the interests of all citizens must do so in a manner that treats all citizens as equals. The problem with a procedure that gives consideration to the racist or sexist views of one citizen is that this has the effect of not treating as equals those citizens who are the objects of such views. This situation poses a dilemma for fair procedural democracy: Should it give consideration to the views of the racist (or the sexist) or to the interests of the individuals who are the object of racist or sexist views? The reason why this is a dilemma is that to give consideration to the interests of either will have the effect of not treating the other as an equal. The egalitarian model of fair procedural democracy seeks to avoid this dilemma by showing that excluding the interests of the racist or sexist from consideration in a democratic decision-making procedure does not treat the individuals who have such interests as less than equals.

We have seen that the neutrality model of fair procedural democracy fails because it lacks a test for distinguishing between interests that should be given consideration in the decision-making procedure and those that should not. The egalitarian model is different from the neutrality model precisely because it does introduce such a test. The general problem with being neutral between interests in a political decision-making procedure is that it ignores the fact that the decisions that are being made are not just for particular individuals but for all citizens; the choices are of a collective or social character. Therefore, if racist or sexist views are given considera-tion in the political decision-making procedure, this entails more than just a particular individual expressing a personal preference for the environ-ment in which he or she would like to live out his or her life; it entails fur-ther a preference for the environment for all citizens of a democratic state in which to live out their lives. A similar point can be made about someone making a claim to some particular liberty such as unrestricted freedom of speech. To give this claim consideration in a political decision-making process means thinking about what it would entail for all citizens to have this unrestricted freedom, not just one particular citizen. Someone might not want to make a claim to unrestricted freedom of speech once he or she has thought out the disadvantages of everyone else also having that free-dom. (Hart 1983: 241–242) The egalitarian model of fair procedural democracy tries to capture this insight in its test for distinguishing be-tween those interests of citizens that should receive consideration and those interests that should not.

This test requires that only those interests which do not threaten the equal worth of any and every citizen are to be given equal considera-tion in a democratic decision-making procedure. (Dworkin 1985: 205; Beitz 1989: ch. 5) Certainly, the substance of this test depends on what we construe to be a threat to a citizen's equal worth. But before dis-cussing that issue, let me first illustrate the intuitive strength of this test. Consider the example of the citizen who professes to have an interest in living in a racist society. This interest fails the test set by the egalitarian model of fair procedural democracy because it is hard to imagine this not threatening the equal worth of those citizens who would be the object of such racist views. (Dworkin 1978: 231) Likewise, sexist views would be a threat to the equal worth of women. Thus, this test does genuinely differentiate the egalitarian and neutrality models of fair procedural democracy.

How do we determine what is a threat to a citizen's equal worth? One approach—a *subjective* approach—would be to say that a threat exists if someone believes that her or his equal worth is threatened. The chief difficulty with this sort of approach is that it seems conceivable that someone could believe that some interest is a threat but be mistaken. Or, conversely, someone might not recognize something as a threat, even though it genuinely is a threat to his or her equal worth. The alternative to a subjective approach is an *objective* approach. An objective approach identifies certain claims and interests as threats to a citizen's equal worth, regardless of whether or not the citizen believes that they are threats. The advantage of such an approach is that it avoids the difficulty of people being mistaken about what is a threat to their equal worth.

Basic to an objective approach is the idea that there are certain conditions or features of a collective decision-making procedure that are necessary for each citizen to enjoy a sense of equal worth. Anything that threatens these conditions or features is logically a threat to a citizen's equal worth. What are these conditions? Although there is a significant amount of controversy about this issue, it is possible to identify at least two conditions that are necessary for each citizen to enjoy a sense of equal worth. (Beitz 1989: 109–116; Dworkin 1988: 19–23) The first condition, perhaps largely symbolic in character, is that each citizen enjoy public status as someone who is worthy of consideration in public deliberations. The second condition is that he or she have the potential to really influence the outcome or decision that can be made; the contrast is to someone enjoying symbolic participation but lacking any genuine chance of making a difference. Only interests that do not threaten these two conditions merit equal consideration under the egalitarian model of fair procedural democracy. The views of the racist, even when they reflect a very small minority opinion, are disqualified because they threaten the symbolic value of each citizen enjoying a worthy public status. But this disqualification does not, in turn, pose a threat to the equal worth of the racist because it does not violate either of the two objectively determined conditions necessary for a sense of equal worth just identified.

So far, the discussion of the egalitarian model of fair procedural democracy has been quite abstract. We have seen that at its core is the principle that a democratic decision-making procedure should give equal consideration to all those interests of different citizens that do not threaten the equal worth of any and every citizen. The practical question is how this principle can be instilled in a political institution. What are the institutional features necessary to realize the egalitarian model of fair procedural democracy? An elementary requirement is an elected decision-making body that operates on some sort of principle of majority rule. Representatives to this body would be chosen in elections that allow everyone to vote. The use of voting in this context would, in the first instance, be a way to ensure that the interests of all citizens are given equal consideration. However, this elected decision-making body would not be unconstrained. It is also necessary for there to be a set of enforceable individual rights on which citizens can stand to ensure that the decision-making procedure does not operate in ways that threaten their equal worth. These are the rights ordinarily associated with existing democratic systems: freedom of speech, freedom of association, freedom of the press, the right to vote and seek office. The nature of these rights will be discussed in some depth in Chapter Four. For now, it is important only to emphasize three points. The first point is that these rights do not exist in order to promote any particular outcome or decision such as the common good or public interest. (This would conflate the distinction between convergent and fair procedural democracy.) The second point is that the egalitarian model of fair procedural democracy inevitably stresses the rights much more than the duties of democratic citizenship. The final point is that although the egalitarian model seems to be rather abstract in character, the rights that flow from it are precisely those that common sense suggests are basic to a democracy.

§4   CONCLUSION

This chapter has dealt with a very complex and difficult question, How should collective decisions be made in a democracy? One of the reasons why this is such a hard question to discuss is the sheer number of different answers political theorists have given to it. My treatment of these different answers has been selective and, for the most part, very critical. I have argued that in the last resort only the egalitarian model of fair procedural democracy offers a promising principle for determining how collective decisions should be made in a democracy. My defense of the egalitarian model has involved two crucial steps. The first step makes the general case for fair procedural democracy over convergent procedural democracy. This case turns on the difficulties of the requirement that a democratic decision-making procedure be designed to converge on policies that serve the common good or public interest. The striking feature of democracy is precisely the lack of certainty about what the outcome or decision will be. (Przeworski 1987: 62; 1991, ch. 1) Fair procedural democracy is attractive because it does not require any specific outcome but instead simply requires that the procedure be fair in its treatment of the *demos* or citizens. The second step explains why the egalitarian model is a better model of fair procedural democracy than the neutrality model. The major point here is that the egalitarian model offers a fairer way to give equal consideration to the interests of the citizens in a democracy. We shall see in the next chapter, however, that although democratic governments do not by their nature necessarily serve any particular end or goal, the authority of the democratic state does nevertheless rest on it acting in conformity with the requirements of social justice.

SUGGESTED READINGS

1. Barber, Benjamin, *Strong Democracy* (Berkeley, University of California Press, 1984). An impressive defense of participatory democracy.
2. Beitz, Charles, *Political Equality: An Essay in Democratic Theory* (Princeton, Princeton University Press, 1989). A superb treatment of the theory and practical implications of what I have called fair procedural democracy.
3. Dahl, Robert, *Democracy and Its Critics* (New Haven, Yale University Press, 1989). The most comprehensive book on contemporary democratic theory.
4. Held, David, *Models of Democracy* (Palo Alto, Stanford University Press, 1987). A useful overview of different theories of democracy, both modern and ancient.
5. Macpherson, C. B., *The Life and Times of Liberal Democracy* (New York, Oxford University Press, 1977). An excellent analytical account of the development of democratic theory since the early nineteenth century.

CHAPTER THREE
Political Obligation

◆

§1 INTRODUCTION

Why should a citizen obey the laws passed by a democratic government? What is it about the collective decisions made by democratic governments that makes them morally binding on their citizens? These are
the questions that we shall be examining in this chapter.

It may, at first sight, be puzzling why political philosophers find
these questions difficult ones. The answer to them appears obvious: we
obey laws in order to avoid being punished; but when there is little risk
of punishment, we disobey the laws. Most people have probably broken
the law at some point in their lives. Who has not driven faster than the
speed limit? Others have likely used illegal drugs such as marijuana or
drunk alcohol while still a minor. Others at some time have probably
not declared all of their income to the government in order to avoid paying additional income tax. The apparent reason why we break the law in
these instances, but not others, is that we realize that the likelihood of
getting caught is pretty slim.

This answer, while having some truth, does not answer the questions
at hand. Although the avoidance of punishment might explain why we *do*
generally obey the law, it does not explain why we *should* obey the law;
and this is the problem that will concern us in this chapter. Ordinarily,
when we think about laws passed by democratic governments, we believe
that we have some sort of moral duty or obligation to obey those laws.
While that duty or obligation may not be absolute and uncompromising,

it is from a moral point of view something which we generally ought to do unless there are very good reasons for not doing so.

Among contemporary legal and political philosophers, there is now a general consensus that in order for individual citizens to have a general moral duty or obligation to obey the laws of a state, the government that makes those rules must have the right to rule. (Raz 1986: ch. 2) The underlying logic is that the existence of the government's right to rule means that we have a general duty or obligation to comply with the collective decisions that it makes. The claim that the government has the right to rule is an issue of the authority of the state: when a government has the authority to make law in a particular jurisdiction, then it can be said to have the right to rule in that jurisdiction, and we can be said to have the general moral duty or obligation to obey that government.

The difficulty for political philosophy is understanding why a government has the authority to make binding political decisions. What gives a government the right to rule over its citizens? Why are individual citizens generally morally bound to obey the laws of a state? These questions raise the general problem of political obligation. (Sometimes philosophers have distinguished between duties and obligations in this context. The treatment of this problem here does not rely on such a distinction, and the terms *duty* and *obligation* are used more or less interchangeably throughout this chapter.) It is frequently argued that there is no compelling answer to the general problem of political obligation. (Wolff 1970; Simmons 1979) Fortunately, our concern in this chapter is with the much narrower, and more manageable, problem of justifying political obligation to a democratic government. What gives a *democratic* government the right to rule over its citizens?

Before we can address this question, it is important to clarify first what kind of right is at issue here. It is possible to distinguish between two different types of rights that might be relevant. (Hart 1984: 83–88; Waldron 1988: ch. 4) *Special* rights are created by a special relationship or transaction between two or more parties and are limited in their scope to those parties. A promise is the paradigmatic example of a voluntary action by an individual that creates a special right. The fact that I promised you something creates for you a special right held against me to fulfill that promise. Special rights are also a standard feature of most sports. For example, during a basketball game, a foul against a player with the ball around the opposing team's hoop creates for that player a special right to make a number of free shots. Special rights can then be represented as conditional rights: their existence requires that a necessary condition be met such as, for example, that there be an antecedent promise or a foul. Distinct from special rights are *general* rights. These

are rights that are enjoyed unconditionally. Such rights are often referred to as "natural" rights. In a legal setting, rights based on private
contracts are standard examples of special rights, whereas the right not
to be physically assaulted is a clear instance of a general right.

Is a democratic government's right to rule *general* or *special*? It is
safe to assume that the right to rule must be a special right. This fact will
be evident after we have considered two basic problems with the idea
that a government could have a general right to rule. The first problem
is that the idea of a general right to rule is inconsistent with the very notion that there can be a problem of political obligation, because it implies
that the authority of the state is in some sense "natural" and, therefore,
does not need to be justified. The second problem raises a commonsense
difficulty with the idea of a general right to rule. The problem of political obligation focuses on the question of why we as individuals have an
obligation to obey the government. It is implied here that we owe this
obligation only to our *own* government, not to all governments. (Simmons 1979: 30–35) No one seriously believes that there is no difference
between our relationship to our own government and to the governments of other countries. Yet if a democratic government's right to rule
is a general right, this would mean that everyone, not just its own citizens, would have an obligation to obey its laws.

As stated previously, the concern of this chapter is with the question, why does a democratic government have a special right to rule?
Questions like this about the source of the authority of the state are not
new. They have perplexed political theorists throughout the history of
Western political thought. In modern political philosophy, however,
two very important parameters have been set on what would count as
an adequate answer to such a question, although the second remains
controversial. (Taylor 1985: 187–210; Green 1988: ch. 6) The first—*the requirement of humanism*—demands that any explanation of the government's right to rule cannot rest on some sort of claim that this right is in
some sense natural or God-given. Instead, the source of the right to rule
must ultimately be either the voluntary actions of the citizens or the benefits generated by the government. The second—*the requirement of individuality*—demands that a defensible theory of political obligation must
explain why the government has the right to rule over each and every
citizen as an individual. A useful way to test whether a theory of political obligation actually meets this second requirement is to try to imagine
being in the position of any citizen and then ask if he or she would find
this a compelling explanation for why he or she should obey the state.
The relevant contrast is to older theories of political obligation, which
tended to focus on explaining why the government has a right to rule
over a particular group of people or nation. The problem with these

older theories is that it is conceivable that an individual citizen might agree that a government has a right to rule over a particular group to which the citizen belongs but nevertheless might deny that she or he finds this a compelling explanation for why she or he as an individual should obey the law of such a government.

These two requirements narrow significantly the possible ways to defend a democratic government's right to rule. We shall distinguish broadly between *citizen-centered* theories of political obligation and *state-centered* theories of political obligation. Citizen-centered theories maintain that the authority of a democratic government can be best understood in light of some sort of action undertaken by each individual citizen. The main idea here is that each citizen does something that generates a special right for a democratic government to rule over him or her. This idea is in contrast to state-centered theories of political obligation, which maintain that something the democratic state does generates its authority to rule over an individual. Ultimately, this chapter argues that the most defensible theory of political obligation is a particular state-centered explanation for why a democratic government has the right to rule over its citizens.

§2.1 CITIZEN-CENTERED THEORIES

Citizen-centered theories of political obligation seek to explain the authority of the democratic state by reference to something that each individual citizen does. For our purposes, we shall focus narrowly on two classes of citizen-based theories of political obligation. These two classes differ over the type of action by the citizen that might be thought to generate a democratic government's right to rule. Consent-based accounts hold that the authority of a democratic state rests on the consent of the citizen. Fairness-based accounts hold that the authority of the democratic state rests on the acceptance of benefits from the state by the citizen. Neither of these two classes of theories of political obligation hold much promise for explaining fully why a democratic government has the right to rule.

§2.2 CONSENT

It was stressed previously that a democratic government has only a special right to rule. Therefore, an adequate theory of political obligation must be able to explain what it is about the special relationship between a democratic government and individual citizens that warrants the government having this special right. The *consent-based* approach to political obligation seizes upon the model of a promise as the paradigm source of a special right. Consider a situation in which I promise to give you $5. The fact that I made this promise to you creates a special right for you against me to give you $5; not everybody has a right against me to give them $5, only those people whom I have promised $5 have this right. The attractiveness of the example of the promise is that it suggests that the source of a special right can be a freely chosen, voluntary act. Theories that adopt the consent-based approach maintain that the source of a democratic government's special right to rule is some sort of freely chosen act by each individual citizen that has a form analogous to a promise.

Before we examine specific consent-based theories of political obligation, it is important to distinguish these theories from the very different idea that a legitimate government is based on a social contract between the government and the people, for the consent-based approach is often confused with this idea of a social contract. The notion that there exists between the government and its citizen body a social contract which should guide the actions of the government is most commonly associated with the political thought of the seventeenth-century English philosopher, John Locke. Often, it has been maintained by those conservative thinkers influenced by Locke that provided that a government complies with the conditions of this contract, it has a right to rule. From a modern perspective, however, this conservative explanation of a government's right to rule is inadequate because it violates what was described above as the *requirement of individuality*. This requirement demands that a theory of political obligation explain why each individual has a moral duty or obligation to obey the government. The social contract notion by itself is unable to provide this explanation; it explains only why a government has the right to rule over a people or a nation as a whole, not why it has a right to rule over specific individuals.

As mentioned previously, theories that adopt the consent-based approach maintain that the source of a democratic government's special right to rule is some sort of freely chosen act by each individual citizen that has a form analogous to a promise. The ideal source of an individual's political obligation to a democratic government, with this approach, would be a promise by each individual citizen to obey the laws enacted by that government. The reality is, however, that in countries which are ordinarily perceived to be democratic to some degree, this sort of promise is never widespread. How many citizens make such a promise? Perhaps landed immigrants, but very few natural citizens, those who were born in a country, have ever made a promise to obey their government. Does this mean that democratic governments in these countries do not have the right to rule? Is it reasonable to require that each and every citizen of a democracy make such a promise before it is legitimate to say that the government has the right to rule? Suppose that one individual citizen simply refuses to make such a promise. Would this refusal mean that a democratic government would not have the authority to rule? How could we structure our political institutions even to give citizens the opportunity to make a promise to obey the government?

Given these problems with the idea that the basis for a democratic government must be a promise made by each individual citizen, most political philosophers sympathetic to the consent-based approach have sought to identify ways, other than by a promise, in which individual citizens might be said to have consented to being ruled by a democratic government. If a promise would constitute a form of *direct* consent to the authority of a government, these alternatives would constitute forms of *indirect* consent to the authority of a democratic government. (Plamenatz 1962: 239) What might be a form of indirect consent that would warrant saying that a democratic government has a right to rule over each and every individual citizen?

The clearest and largely indisputable way in which individuals can consent indirectly to the authority of a democratic government is by taking part in the election process, that is to say, by voting. The general idea is simple. Suppose that an individual citizen votes for candidate X in an open election. It seems very plausible to say that by voting for X, the citizen has consented to obeying laws passed by X. But, more significantly, even if candidate X does not win the election, but instead candidate Y wins, it would seem plausible to say that the voter also has an obligation to obey laws passed by Y. By taking part in the process of electing a candidate, the citizen indirectly consents to accepting the result of the process and obeying the winner, even if the winner is not the citizen's preferred candidate.

The general argument for political obligation to democratic governments based on voting involves three steps. The first step is to say that voting creates for a citizen an obligation to obey laws passed by the winner of the election, whoever the winner is, provided that the winner has fairly won the election. The second step is to emphasize that all democratic governments are characterized by the opportunity for all citizens to vote in elections. As explained in the previous chapter, elections of this sort make sense under the egalitarian model of fair procedural democracy because they are a very practical procedure for giving equal consideration to the interests of all citizens. The third step is to claim that because all citizens have the opportunity to participate in elections for the government, a democratic government can be said to have the right to rule over each and every citizen.

How plausible is this defense of a democratic government's right to rule? At first sight, it seems to have a great deal of plausibility; after all, voting in a fairly run election does seem generally to bind one to the outcome even if it is not an outcome that the voter personally favors. Moreover, this argument seems to demand from democratic governments only that they provide every citizen with the opportunity to vote; this does not seem to be an unreasonable requirement or precondition to demand from any government that seeks the authority to rule. Finally, this defense provides some insight into why there is such widespread commitment to democratic government; because elections are so basic to the very notion of democratic government, it is perhaps the only type of government that can realistically be said to have a right to rule.

Despite these strengths, however, any defense of a democratic government's right to rule based exclusively on the opportunity provided to citizens to vote suffers from a very basic flaw. What about citizens who choose not to vote? Can they be held to an obligation to obey laws made by the winner of the election? Some people who choose not to vote do say something like the following: "Oh well, I don't really care who wins, all of the candidates are acceptable to me so I don't feel any need to vote." This sort of apathetic citizen would seem bound by the outcome of the election. However, other citizens who refuse to vote do so for other reasons. They might say, for example, something like this: "I don't like any of the candidates, and there is no way that I am going to vote for any of them." How, then, can they be said to have an obligation under a consent-based approach to obey laws passed by a government made up of such candidates? The point of not voting for people like this is precisely to express their refusal to consent to being governed by any of the candidates.

This problem of nonvoters may be resolved in a democracy by making voting mandatory. This is the case in Australia, where everyone must vote under federal law. If voting is mandatory, there is no longer the possibility that some citizens might refuse to vote because they do not want to consent to being ruled by any of the candidates in an election. Nevertheless, mandatory voting raises its own problems for a consent-based theory of political obligation. Is it not absurd to say that if people must participate in the electoral process, then their participation can be construed as consent to the outcome of that process?

We have just seen that a defense of a democratic government's right to rule that emphasizes voting as a form of indirect consent to a government breaks down in the case of individuals who do not vote. The problem is that it just is not accurate to interpret their failure to participate in an election as consent to the outcome of that election. The upshot of this problem is that it means that at least some people—those who do not vote in elections—cannot be said to have a moral duty or obligation to obey a democratic government if voting is the only form of indirect consent. This situation then raises the question, are there any other forms of indirect consent?

It is sometimes argued that simply by continuing to live in a country, a person is thereby consenting indirectly to be ruled by the government of that country. The populist version of this argument says, in effect, that if someone does not like it here, that person can leave; and by not leaving, the person is indirectly consenting to the system of government in the country even if the individual does not participate in, for example, the electoral processes of that government.

The difficulties with this argument are strikingly obvious. For most people, their country of residence is where they were born, and there was no initial choice of countries of residence. Moreover, many people do not leave their country of residence because they have no other place to go. In the modern world, with its carefully regulated borders, it is often difficult for people to be accepted as immigrants in many countries. Finally, in certain countries, the dangers of even expressing an interest in emigrating make it hard to see how people's failure to leave can be construed as a form of indirect consent.

§2.3 FAIRNESS

Citizen-centered theories of political obligation emphasize that the source of the authority of the democratic state derives from the actions of its individual citizens. We have just seen that those theories that stress the importance of consent are unable to explain why all citizens are bound by the democratic state's right to rule. The fairness-based theory shifts attention away from the consent of citizens in a democracy to the quite different proposition that the source of political obligation is the acceptance of benefits from the state by each citizen. The main idea here, which shall be referred to as the *principle of fairness,* is that if one accepts benefits in certain social contexts, then that voluntary action generates as a requirement of fair play an obligation to do one's share in the creation or maintenance of those benefits. (Hart 1984: 85–87) The central point is that the democratic state provides certain benefits that each citizen accepts and that this acceptance generates for each citizen a moral duty or obligation to obey the state.

This concrete, everyday example will illustrate the intuitive force of this approach to political obligation: Suppose that Jim and four friends begin to study together for their final exams. Each week, one of the friends prepares detailed notes for the study session and distributes them to everyone else. After four weeks, it is Jim's turn to prepare these notes. Does Jim have an obligation to do so? Suppose that Jim insists that he never promised to prepare the notes. Can we still say that his four friends hold a special right against Jim to prepare the study notes? Presumably, we would argue that Jim has an obligation to his friends because he accepted the benefits of the arrangement; after all, it would be unfair for Jim not to do his part. By analogy, a citizen who accepts benefits from a democratic state has in virtue of that acceptance created for that citizen an obligation to obey the state.

Is this a sound defense of the special right to rule of a democratic government? Criticism of fairness-based accounts of political obligation has had two main strands. One strand has emphasized the limited validity of the principle of fairness. These limits are evident if we consider the case of accepting a gift. Clearly, accepting a gift constitutes accepting a benefit. However, accepting a gift, by its very nature, does not create special rights; gifts are supposed to come with no strings attached. Why is accepting benefits from the state any different from accepting a gift? The other strand of criticism of fairness-based accounts of political obligation focuses on the extent to which a citizen can be said to have accepted benefits provided by the state. The criticism is that the citizen will receive the benefits regardless of what the citizen does, and therefore it is hard to see how receipt of those benefits can generate a moral duty or obligation for the citizen to obey the state that provides those benefits. (Nozick 1974: 90–95)

The principal response to these criticisms has been to elaborate carefully on the nature of the benefits that are provided by the (democratic) state and to explain why these benefits are of a character that warrants the claim that their receipt generates an obligation to the state. (DeLue 1989; Klosko 1992) The central insight of this response has been to stress that among the benefits provided by the state, some of the most important are so-called *public goods*. Public goods are goods that (1) everyone can be presumed to benefit from, (2) require cooperation among a large group of people to produce, and (3) generate benefits from which nobody can be excluded. The paradigmatic examples of public goods provided by the state are law and order, and national defense. The fact that citizens accept from the state the benefits of certain public goods is thought to have an important bearing on the issue of why those citizens can be said to have a moral obligation to the state. The crucial point is that the production of public goods requires the cooperation of a large number of individuals; therefore, unless there is an obligation to the state for all citizens, the state will be unable to provide public goods like national defense and law and order. In other words, you enjoy the benefits of a public good like national defense, it seem only fair that you have some sort of obligation to do your share in the production of that public good.

Although this elaboration and refinement of the fairness-based account of political obligation is an important development, difficulties with the theory that are likely insurmountable still remain. One problem concerns the question of the extent of the obligation on the individual citizen that is established by a focus on the acceptance of public goods. Can this theory justify the sort of redistribution that is characteristic of the modern welfare state in most modern industrial societies? (Klosko 1992: 91; Jacobs 1993a: ch. 3)

Another problem is inherent in the focus on public goods. Theories of political obligation are concerned to show why a government has a special right to rule over its own citizens and not citizens of other countries. Consider, however, the example of the scheme of national defense provided by the government of the United States. The fairness-based theory establishes that because American citizens benefit from the provision of this public good, they can be said to have a moral duty or obligation to the government of the United States to do their share in its provision. However, the benefits of the American defense scheme are enjoyed not only by American citizens; it is undeniable that Canadian citizens living to the north of the United States also enjoy benefits of that scheme. Doesn't it therefore follow on the fairness-based theory that Canadian citizens also have a political obligation to the government of the United States? In other words, the government of the United States enjoys, according to the fairness-based theory, a special right to rule over Canadian citizens in virtue of the fact that it provides Canadians with the benefits of its scheme of national defense.

§3.1   STATE-CENTERED THEORIES

We have seen that the two most prominent citizen-centered theories of political obligation cannot fully justify a democratic state's having a right to rule over its citizens. Now we will turn to state-centered theories of political obligation. An important feature of citizen-centered theories of political obligation is that they raise the prospect that a government can have a right to rule independent of the content of the specific laws it enacts. (Hart 1958: 100) This situation differs from state-centered theories of political obligation. These theories maintain that the special right to rule of a democratic state rests precisely on the sorts of laws and policies that are enacted by that state. The point is that state-centered theo-

`igation hold that the authority of the democratic state
 ₆ the state does rather than on the voluntary action of
 . citizen.

 ⸍centered theories of political obligation differ on what it is
 . democratic government must do to justify its having a special
 ₆nt to rule over its citizens. We shall explore the two most important
state-centered theories. The *utilitarian* theory maintains that individual
citizens have an obligation to obey the state because it serves the general
welfare or utility of our society. The *justice-based* theory maintains that
individuals have a natural duty to obey just institutions that apply to
them. The main idea here is that if a democratic government conforms
to the requirements of social justice, then individuals have an obligation
to obey that government. I shall argue in favor of a justice-based approach to political obligation.

§3.2 THE UTILITARIAN THEORY

Utilitarianism is a doctrine of political morality that has its origins in
eighteenth-century British political thought. The fundamental principle
of utilitarianism is that social and political institutions should be designed so that they achieve the greatest possible utility or welfare in a
society. For our purposes, individual utility or welfare can be understood in terms of either preference-satisfaction or mental states, e.g.,
happiness. The general utility or welfare of a society is determined by
adding up the utility or welfare levels of all individuals who are members of that society.

Utilitarianism has a deep-rooted appeal as a general theory of political morality. After all, surely it does seem plausible to require that a
government act so as to maximize the general welfare of a society. Indeed, this sort of political vision has a very attractive dimension. We
shall see, however, when we begin to examine ideas of rights and social
justice, the limitations of this vision. For now, however, we want to
focus on the idea of a utilitarian theory of political obligation.

The eighteenth-century philosopher David Hume provided the
standard utilitarian theory of political obligation. For Hume, "The general obligation, which binds us to government, is the interest and neces-
sities of society. . . . A small degree of experience and observation suf-
fices to teach us, that society cannot possibly be maintained without the
authority of magistrates, and that this authority must soon fall into con-
tempt where exact obedience is not paid to it." (Hume 1748: 160 &

164–165) The main idea is that maximizing the general utility or welfare requires the existence of society and, without the obedience of citizens to the authority of the state, society could not otherwise subsist.

It is important to distinguish two steps in Hume's argument. The first step is his statement that society cannot subsist without the authority of the state. Some people, though, may doubt the validity of this claim. Many anarchists argue, for example, that the ideal society cannot exist if there is a state. In more concrete terms, it is possible to imagine situations in which the state poses a threat to the continued existence of a given society; the example of the Khmer Rouge in Cambodia in the 1970s comes to mind. For our purposes, though, it is not necessary to challenge Hume's claim that society could not subsist without the authority of the state. It is important only to notice that this claim alone does not constitute an adequate theory of political obligation.

Now we shall consider the second step in Hume's argument. At the beginning of the chapter it was stressed that our concern is to explain why each individual has an obligation to obey the laws of the state; the requirement of individuality reflects this concern. The second step in Hume's statement addresses this requirement. In his reference to "exact obedience," Hume was stressing that in order for the authority of the state to be sustained, it is necessary that every individual obey the state. Here, however, Hume is on weak ground. It is doubtful that the authority of the state will be undermined if one individual does not obey. (Dworkin 1978: 206) Does the existence of some criminal behavior in our society in itself undermine the authority of the state? But then a serious question is raised about how convincing Hume's argument is to each individual. Consider the perspective of an individual who says that although that person accepts that the authority of the state is necessary for the subsistence of society and therefore the general welfare, his or her disobedience by itself does not pose a threat to the continued existence of that authority and, therefore, he or she cannot be said to have an obligation to obey the state. Why shouldn't every individual citizen adopt this perspective? The general point is that the utilitarian theory of political obligation fails to meet the requirement of individuality.

§3.3   THE JUSTICE-BASED THEORY

The utilitarian theory of political obligation breaks down because it is unable to meet the requirement of individuality. Recently, among contemporary political philosophers, there has been a revival of the idea

that the ultimate source of political obligation is a general duty to justice
for each individual. It is my view that the justice-based approach provides the most promise for explaining why a democratic government
has a special right to rule and why each citizen has a moral duty or
obligation to obey the laws of that government. This approach to the
problem of political obligation, which has its origins in medieval theories of natural law and natural right, involves the following reasoning: if
individuals have a natural duty to justice and if a particular state exercises its right to rule in a way that respects the requirements of social
justice, then it is possible to derive from that duty an obligation for individuals to obey that state. (Finnis 1980)

There are numerous recent variations on this justice-based theory
of political obligation. (Rawls 1971: §19, §51; Finnis 1980: 154–156 & chs.
IX–XI; Soper 1984: chs. 2–3; Raphael 1990: 197–204; Waldron, 1993a) The
formulation offered by John Rawls in his extraordinarily influential
book, *A Theory of Justice,* will provide the focus here. According to
Rawls, "... a fundamental natural duty is the duty of justice. This duty
requires us to support and to comply with just institutions that exist and
apply to us. . . . Thus if the basic structure of society is just, or as just as it
is reasonable to expect in the circumstances, everyone has a natural duty
to do his part in the existing scheme." (Rawls 1971: 115) The idea of a
natural duty to justice means that we are required to do something, unconditionally. This idea is in contrast to moral requirements that are
conditional, such as, for example, those requirements that an individual
has in the case of making a promise or, under the principle of fairness,
accepting certain benefits. (See, however, Murphy 1994: 276–277.) How
plausible is it to say that we do have a natural duty to justice? Well, in
many respects, it is almost strikingly self-evident that if there are any
natural duties, there must be a duty to justice. Who could seriously deny
that every individual has a duty to justice? Who could be against justice?

The real debate about a natural duty to justice is not over whether
individuals can be said to have such a duty but is rather over the specific demands of justice since the requirements of a duty to justice are a
function of those demands. The point is that we need to have some idea
of what justice is in order to judge whether or not a set of political institutions serve the interests of justice. The next four chapters are intended to address this issue by identifying certain fundamental features
of an account of justice that will provide a yardstick to judge whether or
not a democratic state respects the requirements of justice. These features will be examined in the light of the most basic values of political
morality, individual liberty, equality, and community. Inevitably, the

discussion of justice will be incomplete. There will be no serious discussion of the place of justice in an ethic of personal morality. Instead, the focus will be narrowly on what political philosophers today call social justice—this is the element of a theory of justice that applies to social and political institutions.

Before turning the discussion to social justice, however, it is necessary first to say a bit more about the justice-based theory of political obligation. Specifically, it is essential to address what many political philosophers regard as the fundamental weakness with the theory. Previously, it was stressed that the political authority of a democratic state involves a special right to rule, as opposed to a general right to rule. The point is that the issue of political obligation revolves around a government having a right to rule over its own citizens, but not the citizens of other states. It is frequently argued, however, that the justice-based theory of political obligation fails to justify a special right to rule; instead, it justifies either a general right to rule or no right to rule at all. (Simmons 1979: 152–156; Dworkin 1986: 193; Klosko 1994: 251–262) The reason is that if everyone has a natural duty to justice and a particular state exercises its right to rule in a fashion that respects the requirements of social justice, then it would seem to follow that everyone would have an obligation to obey that state, not just its own citizens. This criticism has led many modern political philosophers to dismiss any prospects for developing a successful justice-based theory of political obligation.

But it is my view that this criticism rests on a mistake. The source of this mistake is that there has been insufficient attention paid to the exact structure of the argument that underlies the justice-based theory of political obligation. The theory proceeds through two steps. The first step is to postulate that each individual has a natural duty to justice. This duty is necessarily abstract in nature since it does not specify in an exact way the concrete obligations that are implied by it. The second step shifts to the specification of various concrete obligations that can be said to flow from or are derivative from the abstract natural duty to justice. One way to think about these concrete obligations is to focus on institutions that respect the requirements of justice. Consider, for example, private international aid organizations such as OXFAM or Save the Children. These organizations are widely believed to respect the requirements of justice within the realm of the international arena. It follows, then, from the natural duty to justice that individuals might be said to have some sort of moral obligation to support these organizations. A similar argument can be made for a duty on our part to comply with and perhaps support quasi-political institutions such as the International Court of Justice in The Hague. Moreover, the same logic suggests that a democratic state that respects the requirements of justice also generates obligations for individuals.

But it is extremely important to distinguish between two sorts of political obligations to a democratic state that an individual might be said to have under this theory. First, there are obligations for some people that are similar to those they owe to organizations like OXFAM, such as the obligation that many Jewish-Americans feel towards Israel. They believe that the existence of Israel respects the requirements of justice and that, for this reason, they have some sort of duty to sustain its existence. However, this obligation does not presuppose that Israel has authority over these Americans and that, therefore, Israel has a special right to rule over them. Likewise, it is unlikely that anyone would infer from the claim that we have a duty to support OXFAM that OXFAM thus has the right to rule over us. These obligations are what moral philosophers ordinarily call *imperfect* duties; they do not have rights correlated to them. These obligations can be contrasted to *perfect* duties or obligations. Perfect duties give rise to corresponding rights. The justice-based theory of political obligation says that for citizens of a democratic state, if that state exercises its special right to rule in a fashion that respects the requirements of social justice and that if each individual has a natural duty to justice, then those citizens have a perfect duty to obey that state. And the fact that there is this perfect duty explains why the democratic state has a special right to rule over them.

This analysis allows us to formulate more precisely the major criticism of the justice-based theory of political obligation. This criticism says in effect that the theory faces the following dilemma: if all individuals can be said to have a natural duty to justice and if a democratic state respects the requirements of justice, then it follows that all individuals, including the citizens of that state, have *either* an imperfect duty to that state, in which case the state would not have a right to rule, *or* a perfect duty to that state, in which case the state would have a general, as opposed to a special, right to rule, since it would have the right to rule over everyone, not just its own citizens. Yet this formulation also suggests a way to respond to the criticism. Why should only the citizens of the state have a perfect duty to the state based on the natural duty to justice? The answer lies in the link between the state having authority and its respecting the requirements of justice. While organizations like OXFAM can respect the requirements of justice without having a right to rule, the democratic state cannot do so, and, for this reason, it makes sense to ascribe to the state a special right to rule.

Why is it is so important for a democratic government to have a right to rule in order to respect the requirements of justice? The most persuasive answer relates to the sorts of problems of justice that the state resolves. (Finnis 1980: chs. 6–7; Goodin 1989; Waldron 1993a: 22–24) The state is widely perceived among contemporary political philosophers to be a valuable instrument for coordinating collective action among individual citizens so as to achieve certain just ends. (This is a point also emphasized by the fairness-based theory of political obligation.) Consider the example of protecting the environment. This sort of action requires the cooperation and compliance of large numbers of individuals. Without coordination, collective action on the environment would be ineffective. However, without authority, the democratic state would be an ineffective coordinating body, since it would be unable to assure all individuals that they can count on the compliance of everyone else.

§4   CONCLUSION

This chapter has argued that the justice-based theory of political obligation provides the most promising way to answer why each individual should obey the laws of a democratic state. This theory says, in effect, that a citizen has an obligation to obey the democratic state provided that the laws and policies of that state respect the requirements of social justice. (Note, however, that this allows for the possibility that there is a democratic government which conforms to the egalitarian model of fair procedural democracy but does not have the right to make binding collective decisions.) An important consequence of this theory of political obligation is that it shifts attention to questions about social justice and precludes the possibility that the issue of political obligation can be resolved without reference to the substance of the laws and policies of the democratic state. The discussion of social justice in the rest of the book serves, then, to identify not only the form but also the content of the modern democratic vision of politics.

It is important to notice, however, that the justice-based theory of political obligation does not single out democracy as the only form of government that can have a special right to rule. It is conceivable, albeit unlikely, that other forms of government might also respect the requirements of justice, in which case, according to the justice-based theory, their citizens can be said to have a general obligation to obey their laws. The argument in this book does not, therefore, explain why, from a moral point of view, democracy is special, nor does it establish that democracy is the only legitimate form of government. (See Nelson 1980.)

Some readers may be struck by one problem that has not yet been addressed. What if your government does not always respect the requirements of social justice? What then are your obligations under the justice-based approach? These issues are discussed in Chapter Seven.

SUGGESTED READINGS

1. Green, Leslie, *The Authority of the State* (New York, Oxford University Press, 1988). An excellent concise examination of the idea of political authority and its importance to contemporary political theory.
2. Hart, H. L. A., *The Concept of Law* (New York, Oxford University Press, 1961). A seminal book in legal philosophy.
3. Klosko, George, *The Principle of Fairness and Political Obligation* (Lanham, MD, Rowman & Littlefield, 1992). A very sophisticated and spirited defense of the principle of fairness.
4. Nelson, William N., *On Justifying Democracy* (London, Routledge & Kegan Paul, 1980). Although the general theme of this book focuses on why democracy is a form of government preferable to the alternatives, it nevertheless contains many insightful and clear points on the issue of political obligation.
5. Simmons, A. John, *Moral Principles and Political Obligations* (Princeton, Princeton University Press, 1979). The most comprehensive modern analysis of theories of political obligation.

PART TWO

Social Justice

CHAPTER FOUR

The Importance of Rights

———————◆———————

§1   INTRODUCTION

So far, I have argued that the value at the core of democratic government is political equality and that a democratic government's right to rule is contingent on that government's exercising its authority in a manner that is consistent with the requirements of social justice. In this chapter and the three chapters that follow, the more substantial question of how to conceptualize the requirements of social justice will be considered.

Perhaps the most striking characteristic of modern discussions of social justice is the predominance of rights discourse. The requirements of social justice are most commonly expressed in terms of rights. In political debates and the popular media, charges of rights violations and standing on one's rights are treated as the gravest instances of social injustice. Indeed, sometimes it appears that only alleged injustices that can be expressed in terms of rights violations are taken seriously.

Modern philosophers have made an invaluable and distinctive contribution to our understanding of the concept of rights. The purpose of this chapter is to sketch out and evaluate this contribution and relate it to the broader democratic vision of politics. This involves explaining the widespread appeal of the language of rights, the basic function of rights, two types of rights, and what moral rights should be constitutionally protected.

§2   THE APPEAL OF RIGHTS DISCOURSE

Although this fact is often not realized, the language of rights is a relatively new one in our legal and moral discourse. The idea of rights was largely absent from Ancient Greek and Roman moral and political theory. (Finnis 1980: 206–210; Hart 1982: 163) Moreover, it is only in the fifteenth and sixteenth centuries that rights emerged in discussions of ethics and law. Generally, however, it is agreed that the real importance of the concept of rights was revealed in the seventeenth century by the English political theorists Thomas Hobbes and John Locke. Hobbes and Locke are the best-known representatives of the natural rights tradition in political philosophy. Although they differed in important and substantial ways, both Hobbes and Locke urged their readers to imagine the situation of people prior to the existence of government and argued that in such a condition people could be said to have rights. The point is that such rights are natural, as opposed to being contingent on the existence of a particular political and legal system, and have implications for the legitimacy of the existing state.

The value and influence of the natural rights tradition remains controversial. Despite its prominence in the seventeenth century, there was widespread philosophical skepticism about the idea of natural rights by the late eighteenth century. The principal objection raised against the natural rights approach was that it seemed sociologically naive to imagine that anything so elaborate as rights could exist independent of a legal and political system. Hence, the well-known legal and political theorist Jeremy Bentham famously dismissed natural rights as "nonsense on stilts." His contemporary, Edmund Burke, argued that while it is perfectly intelligible to speak of the rights of Englishmen or Americans, he found it incomprehensible that there could be such a thing as 'natural' rights. Building on this style of critique, Karl Marx fifty years later argued that the language of natural rights in effect masks the existing ordering of property relations by representing those relations as natural, rather than sociolegal constructions.

The practical influence of natural rights theory on the French Revolution of 1789 and especially on the American Revolution of 1776 has been less contested. Revolutionaries in both cases appealed to natural rights to justify their rebellions. It is a standard observation that the Declaration of Independence is steeped in the language of natural rights. Moreover, the Bill of Rights amended to the 1789 Constitution is ordinarily thought to reflect almost exclusively this tradition of political thought. Recently, however, historians of the American Revolution have begun to question this view of the ideological origins of the Revolution as being too simplistic. (Bailyn 1967; Pocock 1975) Increasingly, doubts have been raised about the importance and influence of the idea of natural rights. Instead, the Revolution has been viewed through the lens of liberty. The point is that what allegedly motivated the American Revolution was a concern about the threat British rule posed to liberty. However, it is important to recognize that the idea of liberty at stake here is not one easily reconciled with the natural rights tradition but rather one that has its origins in the civic humanist and republican tradition stemming from Machiavelli, a tradition that was overtly hostile to natural rights.

The implications of these two controversies are significant. The objection that natural rights are misconceived raises the issue of why we should bother to talk about natural rights. A typical response is that even if natural rights are misconceived, they have been profoundly influential in the founding of the United States. But the historical controversy just noted questions that interpretation of the American Revolution, in which case maybe we don't really need the language of natural rights at all.

The odd thing about the idea of natural rights is, in my view, that it has persisted despite this widespread hostile reception. What is it about the idea that makes it so attractive for expressing concerns about social justice? What makes rights so special in the conceptual arsenal of philosophical analysis of social justice?

Ultimately, the appeal of rights discourse is its explicit potential for criticizing existing political and legal institutions and practices. Seventeenth century rights theorists such as Hobbes and Locke explicitly appeal to natural rights in order to identify a standard for judging political institutions that exists independently of those institutions. The salient contemporary distinction is between *moral* and *legal* rights. Moral rights, as distinct from legal rights, can be said to exist independently of a particular legal system. Moral rights can provide, in this respect, a viewpoint from which legal and political institutions and practices can be judged. Consider, for example, the widely held view that everyone has a right not to be tortured. Even if a government does not legally prohibit the torture of, say, political prisoners and that therefore the prisoners cannot be said to have a legal right not to be tortured, torture can still be condemned on the grounds that it violates those prisoners' moral rights.

This critical role of moral rights fits well with the role of require-ments of social justice in a democratic society. As the well-known legal philosopher Ronald Dworkin puts it,

> It is part of our common political life, if anything is, that justice is our critic not our mirror, that any decision about the distribution of any good—wealth, welfare, honors, education, recognition, office—may be reopened, no matter how firm the traditions that are then challenged, that we may always ask of some settled institutional scheme whether it is fair. (Dworkin 1985: 219)

Although the language of moral rights provides us with an avenue for the promotion of this critical role for justice, it may not be the only such road. For critics of rights discourse, however, the challenge is to map out an alternative method to criticize the status quo. At present, though, those efforts are still in their infancy. Moreover, many political philosophers and indeed most ordinary citizens and public officials find it more convenient to use and adapt the discourse of rights.

§3   THE FUNCTION OF RIGHTS

Although the concept of rights has enjoyed wide currency for nearly five hundred years, modern political and legal philosophers have nonethe-less advanced considerably our understanding of the concept of rights. These advances have been largely the consequence of careful analysis of the moral and legal practice of rights. The most important objective of this analysis, for our purposes, has been to clarify the distinctive role that rights can play in the political morality of a democratic state. It is worth emphasizing, however, that the exact meaning of a right varies, depending on the context, and that the discussion here is intended only to illuminate the concept of rights in the democratic vision of politics.

At the core of this concept of rights is the idea that having a right is in some sense to the advantage of the right-holder, for having a right warrants respect from others and can be the basis for making claims against them. This idea of a right being a type of advantage has been at the center of debates about the nature and importance of rights since the concept was first introduced. Rights theorists have long disagreed, how-ever, about how rights function as an advantage for their holder.

What is the nature of the advantage rights involve? How do rights function to advantage their holders? There are two distinct perspectives from which these questions can be approached, and both have generated significant debate among legal and political philosophers. The first perspective is in terms of what having a right means to the right-holder. Most analyses of this perspective have first focused on legal rights and then have sought to extend the results to moral rights. In effect, two competing theories about what a legal right means to the right-holder have prevailed. One theory (which is generally labeled the *choice* theory of rights) holds that what having a right means to the right-holder is that he or she has a "legally respected choice." (Hart 1982: 189) The main idea is that when a legal obligation or duty for a person is correlated to the right of someone else, the result is that someone else—the right-holder—can waive that duty or alternatively demand that it be fulfilled. The point is that ultimately it is the choice of the right-holder to decide whether or not that duty or obligation is binding. Consider, for example, the legal rights of ownership if you own a house. Those ownership rights mean that other people have a duty or obligation not to enter your house. Ultimately, of course, you can choose to waive that duty for some people and in effect give them permission to enter your house. In other words, according to the choice theory of rights, to enjoy legal rights of ownership in a house means that you have a legal respected choice about who and when the duties and obligations of others with regard to that house are binding. Rights, therefore, function as an advantage for their holders because they protect their realm of choice.

The other theory (which is generally called the *benefit* theory of rights) holds that having a right is to the advantage of the right-holder because he or she will benefit from others respecting that right. (Lyons 1979: chs. 1 & 5; MacCormick 1978; Raz 1986: ch. 7) Most defenders of the benefit theory point out obvious shortcomings with the choice theory of rights. There are, for example, numerous rights that seem not to involve respect for the choices of the right-holder. A child's right to education, for instance, is generally thought to be compatible with a compulsory requirement that he or she attend school, meaning that the child cannot waive his or her education. Similarly, most legal systems allow individuals to waive minor physical assaults on their bodies but do not allow them to waive major physical assaults. The idea is that you can allow someone to, say, pierce your ear but that you cannot allow someone to kill you. If the choice theory of rights is correct, it would follow, contrary to common sense, that while you have a right not to be subject to minor physical assaults like ear piercing, you do not have a right not to be subject to major physical assaults like being killed. What defenders of the benefit theory of rights seize on is that in the case of both education and physical assault, the issue is really a question of what benefits the right-holder and not of whether or not a legally respected choice is at stake. Having the right to education means that the right-holder will benefit from receiving an education. Likewise, the right not to be physically assaulted presupposes that the right-holder will benefit from not being assaulted. Of course, some minor physical assaults like ear piercing may be to one's benefit, provided they are consensual. In contrast, it is hard to imagine that a major physical assault like being killed would ever be to someone's benefit! The point is that the benefit theory of rights is better able to explain certain rights than is the choice theory.

Proponents of the choice theory typically point out that the benefit theory also has problems. An important problem is that many well-known rights can be exercised in ways that seem not to benefit the right-holder. Consider, for example, a case in which a person has $10,000. This situation means, in effect, that it is that person's right to spend the $10,000 however she wants. Clearly, though, she can thus spend it in foolish ways or simply give it away to people who do not need it. The result is that having the right to spend the money will not in fact necessarily benefit her or at least will not benefit her as much as if she had, for example, been forced to save some of it. Another important objection to the benefit theory of rights is that it seems to make the reference or appeal to rights redundant. The logic of the objection is that if all rights do is signify that something will benefit the right-holder, why bother to make reference to rights at all instead of simply saying that doing so-and-so benefits someone. In other words, the benefit theory has a difficult time explaining why rights are indispensable and special.

We have just seen that both the choice and the benefit theories of rights face serious objections. Neither seems to provide an adequate account of why having a right is to the advantage of the right-holder. Which of these two theories should then be embraced? Among modern political philosophers, there is an increasing hesitation to embrace either. Instead, more and more political philosophers seem to think that both theories adopt a mistaken perspective on the importance of rights in a vision of political morality (Nozick 1974; Dworkin 1978; Waldron 1993c; Jacobs 1993a). Both the choice and the benefit theories try to analyze rights from the perspective of the right-holder by asking what having a right means to the right-holder. This sort of perspective is said to be mistaken, however, because in a vision of political morality, the real advantage of having a right is what it means to people other than the right-holder, specifically, those against whom the right is held. The main idea is that if you really want an adequate analysis of how rights function as an advantage for the right-holder, you must approach it from the perspective of those against whom the right is held, and not from the perspective of the right-holder.

What is the importance of rights to those against whom they are held? For example, what is the significance of individual rights held against the government? What do rights such as the right to free speech mean to the government? These questions shift attention away from the debate between the choice and the benefit theories of rights. Instead, these questions emphasize that an important function of rights in political morality is that rights set constraints on what governments can do and that rights narrow the range of possible goals they can pursue or even can sometimes set.

Here is an example to illustrate this perspective. Suppose that a group of Nazis decided that they wanted to assemble together and publicly express their deeply repugnant political views. If there were no moral or legal rights involved, it would seem appropriate and justified for a democratically elected government to prohibit the Nazis from assembling and expressing their views. After all, because such a prohibition would generally reflect the views of the overwhelming majority, ordinarily this would be sufficient to justify the government's action. However, if we admit that rights might be involved, the scenario becomes much more complicated. Suppose that we accept that everyone has the right to freedom of speech and freedom of assembly. What does this mean for a government prohibition on the Nazis' assembling and publicly expressing their views? When no rights are assumed, such a prohibition is easily justified. However, once we acknowledge that everybody including the Nazis, have certain rights, then it becomes much more difficult, if not impossible, to justify such a prohibition. Thus, the rights signify realms where government measures that might otherwise be easily justified need very special and careful justification. The relevant point is that the rights to freedom of speech and freedom of assembly are to the advantage of the Nazis, not in the sense that they protect their choices or promote their interests but rather in the sense that those rights constrain how the government and others can treat them.

The most influential account of this perspective on rights has been provided by Ronald Dworkin in his book *Taking Rights Seriously*. According to Dworkin,

Individual rights are political trumps held by individuals. Individuals have rights when, for some reason, a collective goal is not a sufficient justification for denying them what they wish, as individuals, to have or to do, or not a sufficient justification for imposing some loss or injury upon them. That characterization of a right is, of course, formal in the sense that

> it does not indicate what rights people have or guarantee, indeed, that they have any. But it does not suppose that rights have some special metaphysical character. (Dworkin 1978: xi)

Dworkin's image of rights as trumps is powerful because it emphasizes that in politics, rights function to restrict rather than to motivate ordinary political decision-making. Rights in this sense are valuable because they constrain government rather than because of what they mean to the right-holder.

This perspective on rights suggests why the language of rights is so useful for expressing concerns about social justice. The central issue in any theory of social justice in a democratic state is the problem of unequal relations between people. (Barry 1989: 3) The reason is that democracies are, as we saw in Chapter Two, founded on a commitment to political equality, and yet existing democratic states are characterized by many different forms of inequality. What political philosophers try to explain is which forms of inequality are fair and why. For example, they consider when inequalities in wealth are justified and why. Rights function to identify forms of inequalities that are hard to justify. When a political decision involves such an inequality, a right acts as a trump on that decision, in the sense that it demands an extraordinary justification, and not just one that appeals to the general welfare or the public interest.

This perspective on rights also fits well with the theory of political obligation defended in the previous chapter. There, I argued that ultimately the most defensible theory for holding citizens to an obligation to obey the laws of a democratic state is a justice-based one. A justice-based theory of political obligation says that for citizens of a democratic state, if that state exercises its special right to rule in a fashion that respects the requirements of social justice and each individual has a natural duty to justice, then those citizens have a perfect duty to obey that state. The virtue of an understanding of social justice that is expressed in terms of rights as trumps is that the requirements that a democratic state must meet in order to ground its authority are clear and accessible.

§4   DEMOCRATIC RIGHTS

Rights have just been characterized as a "trump" on political decision-making by democratic governments. The main idea is that rights matter because from the perspective of the government and from those other than the right-holder, rights set constraints on what can be done. Rights in this sense identify inequalities that need special justification.

For our purposes, it is possible to distinguish between two general types of moral rights, *democratic rights* and *entitlement rights*. Democratic rights are those equal rights that all citizens should have to participate in the democratic political process. Entitlement rights are those equal rights that all citizens should have to the benefits and burdens of their shared social life. The concept of entitlement rights will be discussed in the next section. Here, we shall focus on democratic rights.

The importance of democratic rights is evident from our discussion of models of democracy in Chapter Two. There, it was argued (in §3.3) that the most innovative and defensible model of democracy is the egalitarian version of fair procedural democracy. At the core of that model of democracy is the principle that a democratic decision-making procedure should give equal consideration to all those interests of different citizens that do not threaten the equal worth of any and every citizen. Democratic rights function to ensure equal consideration of the interests of everyone in democratic decision-making.

There are a number of different democratic rights, including the right to vote, the right to run for political office, the right to free speech, and the right to assemble for political purposes. All of these are equal rights in the sense that all citizens enjoy them to the same degree. Nobody has more of a right to vote or run for political office than anybody else. Although all of these rights are familiar, the nature and scope of each is controversial. The right to vote and the right to free speech have both been carefully scrutinized by modern political philosophers.

The right to vote is perhaps the best known example of a democratic right. The idea is that all citizens in a democracy have an equal right to vote so that they can have their interests represented in the legislative assemblies where political decisions are made. Inequalities in voting are never justified, each citizen's right to vote would trump any attempt to distribute votes unequally. Despite the familiarity of the right to vote, there is surprisingly little agreement over what constitutes an equal right to vote. The reason is that voting in a democracy is important because of its link to representation, but it is controversial what the character of that link should be. Consider the following two questions: Does an equal right to vote mean that the vote of each voter should count exactly as much as the vote of any other voter in the country? Does an equal right to vote also mean that racial and ethnic minorities should be guaranteed the election of minority representatives? The first question raises the issue of "quantitative" equality in voting rights. The second question raises the issue of "qualitative" equality in voting rights. (Beitz 1989: ch. 7)

The issue of "quantitative" equality in voting rights has been addressed by the U.S. Supreme Court in a number of landmark decisions, most notably, the two 1964 decisions, *Wesberry v. Sanders* and *Reynolds v. Sims*. In these cases, the Supreme Court adopted the idea of creating equally populated electoral districts so that each voter, no matter where the voter lived, would have a vote that counted as much as the vote of anyone else. The reasoning was that if electoral districts varied in terms of the number of registered voters, this variation would mean that some people's votes—those in districts with fewer registered voters—would have more of an impact on the outcome than other people's votes and, in this sense, would count for more in the election of representatives.

The debate over "qualitative" equality in voting rights has been at the center of the civil rights movement in the United States. (Abraham 1967: ch. 7; Thernstrom 1987) Despite the enactment of the Civil War Amendments to the Constitution—in particular the Fifteenth, which specifies that the "right to citizens of the United States to vote shall not be denied or abridged by the United States or any State on account of race, color, or previous condition of servitude"—there undoubtedly was widespread racial discrimination in voter registration in a number of southern states until at least the mid-1960s. In Mississippi in 1965, for example, a mere 6.7 percent of eligible black voters were registered to vote. The Voting Rights Act, passed in 1965, was designed explicitly to remove racial barriers to voter registration such as literacy tests and poll taxes. The rationale was that such barriers constitute violations of the right to vote. The impact of the Voting Rights Act was immediate and dramatic. In the space of two years in Mississippi, for example, the registration of black voters increased ninefold. By 1967, nearly 60 percent of eligible black voters were registered.

Now, the debate has shifted away from whether barriers to voting registration violate the right to vote—they certainly do!—to whether the right to vote is compromised when electoral districts function to ensure that black voters do not make up a majority of the electorate and, therefore, are unlikely to elect (and have not elected) a representative from their own community. The point is that despite increased voter registration, the gerrymandering of electoral districts can deny black voters representation from their own community. The substantial question is whether denial of representation constitutes a violation of the equal right to vote of citizens of the United States.

One view is that an equal right to vote means simply that all citizens, regardless of their race or gender, can vote. This view holds that the right cannot mean that each citizen's vote will actually make a difference, and cannot mean that the representative you prefer will be elected. In other words, the equal right to vote is said not to require "qualitative" equality in voting rights.

Others argue, however, that this view ignores the importance of the connection between voting and being represented in political decision-making. If literacy tests and poll taxes constitute barriers that violate the equal right to vote, so too must electoral districting that functions to prevent minorities from having their representatives elected. Their point is that it seems arbitrary to try to restrict the scope of the right to vote simply to equal access to register to vote.

Principled disagreements over the right to free speech have been even more pronounced. As a democratic right, the importance of free speech seems obvious in the sense that it facilitates open, critical discussion of public policy and enables people to express freely their views on political decisions and decision-makers. This is certainly how the right was originally developed in the English Bill of Rights of 1688. Moreover, it explains the traditional relation between the right to free speech and the sacredness of freedom of the press in a democracy.

An important issue in competing theories of free speech is whose right is at stake. The traditional view is that the speaker is the right-holder because he or she needs the protection afforded the right so that he or she can freely express his or her opinions. The principal difficulty with this traditional view is that it is then hard to explain how, for example, a newspaper can refuse to publish all of the letters it receives without violating the right to free speech of the people who wrote the letters. An alternative view, associated in particular with Madison, is that the real right-holders are the listeners, not the speaker, and that the right to free speech guarantees that they are exposed to controversial ideas. (Scanlon 1972, 1979) The point is that when we think about regulating and categorizing speech, we should think about it from the perspective of the listener rather than the speaker.

The more substantial debates have been over what is protected by the right to free speech. Does a Nazi have a right to express anti-Semitic opinions that reflect racial hatred? Do members of the Ku Klux Klan have the right to burn crosses? Do high school students have the right to wear a black armband that signifies sympathy for the Black Panthers? Does a teacher have the right to deny publicly that the Holocaust ever happened?

Perhaps the most discussed example of when free speech can be regulated arises in the case of pornography. Traditionally, perspectives on the relation between pornography and free speech are divided between the conservative and liberal camps. So-called conservatives argued that because pornography is morally debased and contrary to the traditional moral standards of the community, it should be censored. (Kristol 1971) In response, liberals have insisted that even if pornography is indeed morally debased, the censorship of it infringes on free speech. Their claim, then, is that looking at pornography involves a right to do the morally wrong thing. (Dworkin 1985: ch. 17; Jacobs 1993a: 77–79 & 129–135)

Recently, and especially in the past ten years, a new perspective on pornography has been forged by some feminists. (Mackinnon 1987, 1994; Itzin 1992) These antipornography feminists advance two principal and related claims. The first claim is that pornography is detrimental to the realization of gender equality. Their point is that what is wrong with pornography is its effects on equality and not that it is contrary to the traditional moral standards of the community. The second claim is that legal institutions should be used to mitigate against the detrimental effects of pornography. While both of these claims are controversial, it is the second claim that has provoked the most critical response and outrage, for it has appeared to many that antipornography feminism calls for the nullification of the right to free speech. (Strossen 1995)

Perhaps the most cogent response to this criticism is that it misrepresents what antipornography feminists find objectionable about pornography, namely, that it silences women. (Langton 1993) The relevant point is that in order to promote freedom of speech for all, it is necessary to censor pornography either by enacting the criminal law or by allowing for civil suits that would enable victims of pornography to sue the producers and distributors of pornography for damages. The main idea, then, is that, contrary to what their critics say, it is the antipornography feminists who are the "true" defenders of freedom of speech and that it is the (liberal) defenders of a right to pornography who threaten it. Ultimately, of course, the strength of this perspective depends on an account of how pornography can be said to silence women, and many remain skeptical that a convincing account will be forthcoming. (Dworkin 1991; Jacobson 1995)

§5   ENTITLEMENT RIGHTS

Entitlement rights are those equal rights that all citizens have to the benefits and burdens of their shared social life. The underlying idea is that the formation of a society results in the production of important and valuable benefits and burdens. A theory of social justice addresses the question of how some of those benefits and burdens should be distributed among individuals. (Not all of the benefits and burdens of social life are necessarily distributed among assignable individuals. For example, many cultural benefits such as a rich history do not have a character that makes it appropriate to talk about their distribution among individuals.)

There are in modern political philosophy many competing theories of social justice. These different theories reflect opposing views about what is a just distribution of the benefits and burdens of social life and what are the appropriate mechanisms for judging that distribution. We shall in the next three chapters explore some of the main differences with respect to the distribution of the three most visible and valued benefits of social life. These are individual liberty, wealth and economic resources, and the goods of community.

Despite the emphasis in subsequent chapters on disagreements among political philosophers over questions of social justice, it is important to realize that these disagreements often mask substantial agreement among the most influential theorists of social justice. (Sen 1992: 1–30) The point of agreement is that social justice in a democracy requires that all citizens enjoy by some measure equal rights to individual liberty, economic opportunities, and community. What they disagree on is the domain and scope of those equal rights.

This consensus on the treatment of the concept of social justice in modern political philosophy is reinforced by the profound and dominant influence of the American political philosopher John Rawls. Rawls in his 1971 book, *A Theory of Justice*, advanced and defended a theory of social justice (which he calls "justice as fairness") organized around the general belief that, "all social primary goods—liberty and opportunity, income and wealth, and the bases of self-respect—are to be distributed equally unless an unequal distribution of any or all of these goods is to the advantage of the least favored." (Rawls 1971: 303) Rawls's theory of justice has become the benchmark of comparison for all other theories of social justice. As Robert Nozick has put it, "Political philosophers now must either work within Rawls's theory or explain why not. . . . Even those who remain unconvinced after wrestling with Rawls's systematic vision will learn much from closely studying it. . . . It is impossible to read Rawls's book without incorporating much, perhaps transmuted, into one's own deepened view." (Nozick 1974: 183)

The specific elements of Rawls's theory of justice as fairness are neatly captured by the following two principles:

First Principle: Each person is to have an equal right to the most extensive system of equal basic liberties compatible with a similar system of liberty for all.

Second Principle: Social and economic inequalities are to be arranged so that they are both

(a) to the greatest benefit of the least advantaged. . . .
(b) attached to offices and positions open to all under conditions of fair
   equality of opportunity. (Rawls 1971: 302)

The importance of these two principles is that they set out Rawls's view
about how the benefits and burdens of social life should be distributed
among individuals in a democratic society. In effect, Rawls maintains
that each individual should have an equal entitlement right to the same
liberties, should have an equal right to compete under conditions of fair
play for valuable opportunities in society, and that with respect to other
advantages the distribution should function to maximize the situation of
the worst-off in society.

   We shall examine Rawls's theory in more depth in subsequent
chapters. It is worth noting here, however, that political philosophers
have disagreed not only with his views about the specific entitlement
rights individuals should have in a democratic society but also about the
way in which Rawls justifies his own particular theory, especially his
appeal to a hypothetical social contract. (See, for example, Daniels 1989.)
Although these disagreements about how to justify a specific theory of
social justice are extraordinarily important, because this book is only an
introduction to political philosophy it provides only a cursory examination of that debate.

   The notion of entitlement rights is designed, then, to highlight both
the agreement and disagreement among modern political philosophers
over the nature of social justice. Democratic rights identify those goods,
like votes, which are the same for everyone. Entitlement rights denote
those goods—the benefits and burdens of social life—to which all citizens have an equal right but about which there is substantial disagreement among political philosophers over the exact proportion or procedure for determining how much of those goods each citizen is entitled.

§6   WHICH RIGHTS (IF ANY) SHOULD BE
CONSTITUTIONALLY PROTECTED?

Although many modern political philosophers hold the view that individuals have important moral rights that function to trump what democratic governments ought to do, most are sensitive to the point that not
all moral rights should be constitutionally protected. For example, while
most of us think that we have a moral right to be told the truth by our
friends, few of us believe that such a right should be constitutionally enshrined and enforced through legal institutions. There is, then, an im-

portant distinction between *moral* rights and *constitutional* rights. (Dworkin 1978: ch. 4) In political morality, the moral rights are the democratic rights that individuals should have for the sake of fair procedural democracy, and the entitlement rights that individuals can be said to have as a requirement of social justice. Constitutional rights, in contrast, are those institutional rights of positive law that are enshrined in the constitution and are administered by the courts.

This distinction between moral and constitutional rights is of fundamental importance to modern democratic theory, because constitutional rights require the courts or an independent judiciary composed of unelected judges to have the political power and legal authority to nullify laws enacted by elected legislative assemblies. The legal practice of the courts having the authority to nullify laws passed by elected legislatures like Congress is called *judicial review*. The basic issue of political morality raised by the idea of constitutional rights is whether judicial review is consistent with democracy. There are four broad positions that have been taken on this issue.

The first position is to deny that there should be any constitutionally enshrined rights in a democracy. The main reason is that because constitutional rights require judicial review and the practice of judicial review allows for the nullification of legislation passed by democratically elected governments, it is inconsistent to have such rights in a democracy. Rights on this view should be determined by democratically elected representatives of the people. (Waldron 1993b; Wolin 1996) The upshot of this viewpoint is that much of the activity of the U.S. Supreme Court in this century appears undemocratic.

The second position says that although there should be some constitutional rights in a democracy, the only constitutionally enshrined rights should be democratic rights, that is to say, those equal rights that all citizens should have to participate in the democratic political process. (Ely 1980) The logic of this position is to say, in effect, that you cannot rely on majoritarian legislative assemblies to protect and promote the democratic rights of minorities when presumably those minorities seek to influence and change the decisions made by those assemblies. The point is that you need an independent judiciary to ensure that all citizens, especially those who are members of vulnerable minorities, have an equal right to participate in electoral politics and influence representatives. Notice, though, that this perspective denies to courts the role of protecting entitlement rights.

The third position says that both the democratic and entitlement rights of vulnerable minorities should be constitutionally protected. (Dworkin 1985: ch. 2; 1990) The reasoning is that neither class of rights is

safe from the excesses of legislative assemblies that operate in the interests of the majority. There is, in other words, no basis for thinking that
democratic rights should be subject to judicial review but entitlement
rights should not. What ultimately motivates any defense of judicial review is fear of the so-called "tyranny of the majority," and it seems
likely that, without the prospect of judicial nullification, this tyranny
will affect not just political opportunities but also the fair distribution of
the benefits and burdens of social life.

The fourth position stems from worries about the excesses of the
third position. (Bork 1990) The claim that the courts should protect the
democratic and entitlement rights of vulnerable minorities allows for
the possibility of an active Supreme Court nullifying popular legislation
and substituting legislation of its own that is unpopular among the vast
majority of citizens. The problem, then, is that assigning the protection
of constitutional rights to the courts provides the courts with the opportunity to invent rights that will in turn constrain what can be done by
democratically elected officials. How do we embrace constitutional
rights while preventing the courts from inventing rights?

The fourth position on judicial review holds, then, that the only
constitutional rights that should be recognized by the courts are those
originally intended by the drafters of the constitution. In the United
States, for example, it would follow that if the Founding Fathers didn't
intend a certain right, then it can't be the case that others today have a
right. What worries many of the critics of the "original intentions" is
how we know what were the intentions of the Founding Fathers and
why those intentions are at all binding on us today. (Arthur 1995: ch. 1)

§7   CONCLUSION

This chapter has explained that the widespread appeal of rights discourse derives from the potential of moral rights for criticizing existing
political and legal institutions and practices. The innovative feature of
modern political philosophy has been the emphasis on rights as a side
constraint or "trump" on the political decisions of elected representative
assemblies. Two types of rights have been identified as especially important to the political morality of the modern democratic state. Democratic rights are those equal rights that all citizens should have to participate in the democratic political process. Entitlement rights are those
equal rights that all citizens should have to the benefits and burdens of
their shared social life. Modern theories of social justice differ principally over which entitlement rights individuals in a democracy can be

said to have. The rest of this book addresses those disagreements with respect to the three values—individual liberty, economic equality, and community—that are generally regarded as the core of any plausible theory of social justice.

SUGGESTED READINGS

1. Dworkin, Ronald, *Taking Rights Seriously* (Cambridge, MA, Harvard University Press, 1978). The most influential book on theories of rights written by a modern legal and political philosopher.
2. Waldron, Jeremy, editor, *Theories of Rights* (New York, Oxford University Press, 1984). A superb collection of the most influential philosophical essays on rights written over the past fifty years.
3. Thernstrom, Abigail, *Whose Votes Count?* (Cambridge, MA, Harvard University Press, 1987). An interesting and informative account of voting rights in the United States and their implication for democratic theory and practice.
4. Arthur, John, *Words That Bind: Judicial Review and the Grounds of Modern Constitutional Theory* (Boulder, Westview Press,1995). An excellent assessment of the philosophical foundation of various theories of judicial review.
5. Nozick, Robert, *Anarchy, State, and Utopia* (New York, Basic Books, 1974). After Rawls, probably the single most influential book in political philosophy in the past twenty-five years.

CHAPTER FIVE
The Place of Liberty

◆

§1 INTRODUCTION

Modern democracies are closely associated with individual freedom or
liberty. (I use these two terms more or less interchangeably.) Among
modern political philosophers, important questions revolve around explaining the link between freedom and democracy. Some of these questions stem from the difficulty of defining freedom and showing what
distinguishes freedom from other things we value. Other questions stem
from disagreements over the role and place of individual liberty in a
democracy. These disagreements reflect differences over why we value
individual liberty and how much we value freedom in comparison with
other goods like economic equality and community.

In modern political philosophy, there has been a marked shift
away from addressing questions about the way to define freedom towards questions about the place of individual liberty in a democracy.
The reason for this shift is probably that there are growing doubts about
there being one simple definition of liberty or freedom. Instead, freedom
appears to be an "essentially contested concept" in the sense that the
way in which different political philosophers define it is a function of
their views about the importance of individual liberty and its place in a
democracy. (Gallie 1956; Gray 1978; Connolly 1983) The point is that, on
reflection, the more fundamental philosophical questions about individual liberty are about its conceptual role in the democratic vision of politics, rather than the way it is defined.

This chapter examines the debates around individual liberty in modern political philosophy. At the center of these debates is the idea that individuals can be said to have, as a requirement of social justice, a general right to liberty. Some of the most innovative recent political philosophy challenges the cogency of such an entitlement right to liberty in the context of democratic political morality. This chapter explains the decline of the general right to liberty in recent political philosophy and the increased emphasis instead on rights to basic liberties.

§2 THE GENERAL RIGHT TO LIBERTY

In the history of political thought, the most influential and best known examination of individual liberty was provided by the nineteenth-century English philosopher, John Stuart Mill, in his famous essay *On Liberty*, published in 1859. Practically all modern philosophical defenses of individual liberty explicitly acknowledge an intellectual debt to Mill. Mill made two especially important claims about how we should view the relationship between democracy and freedom. The first claim is that we should not be complacent about threats to freedom in a democracy. Although democratic revolutions such as the American Revolution were generally motivated by a concern for liberty, in practice democracies operate predominantly through majority rule and indeed are distinctive among types of government because of their emphasis on majority rule. This raises, however, the prospect of what Mill describes, following Tocqueville, as "the tyranny of the majority." His point is that in a democracy the freedom of eccentric individuals and unpopular minority groups is at risk of being curtailed by laws that reflect the views of the majority. (Mill 1859: 7–9)

The second important claim Mill makes is that the freedom at risk in a democracy is what he calls "individual independence." (Mill 1859: 9) By this, he means the freedom of individuals to form and hold opinions and "to carry these [opinions] out in their lives, without hindrance, either physical or moral, from their fellow men [sic], so long as it is at their own risk and peril." (Mill 1859: 62) The relevant contrast is between freedom as individual independence and freedom as republican self-rule. The latter type of freedom is the freedom of an individual to participate in politics and make the rules that collectively govern her or his society. In a democracy, under Mill's analysis, freedom as republican self-rule is unproblematic and not seriously under threat because all democracies institutionalize democratic rights, such as the right to vote, which protect and promote this kind of freedom. Hence, Mill concerns

himself with the protection and promotion of freedom as individual independence in a democracy.

Mill famously defends "one very simple principle" for the treatment of freedom as individual independence in a democracy:

> That principle is, that the sole end for which mankind are warranted, indi-
> vidually or collectively, in interfering with the liberty of action of any of
> their number, is self-protection. That the only purpose for which power
> can be rightfully exercised over any member of a civilized community,
> against his will, is to prevent harm to others. His own good, either physi-
> cal or moral, is not a sufficient warrant. . . . The only part of the conduct of
> any, for which he is amenable to society, is that which concerns others. In
> the part which merely concerns himself, his independence is, of right, ab-
> solute. Over himself, over his own body and mind, the individual is sover-
> eign. (Mill 1859: 14)

What exactly Mill means here is a matter of considerable debate among
philosophers and historians, although there can be little doubt that the
principle Mill advocates is anything but "very simple."

For our purposes, the important legacy of Mill is in terms of laying
the groundwork for the dominant paradigm for thinking about the relation between individual liberty and democracy among political philosophers for much of the twentieth century. This dominant paradigm holds
that individuals have a moral right to do what they want, provided they
do not harm others. The central idea is that democratic governments,
like all other forms of government, are required by justice to respect this
general right of individuals to be free, and thus they are significantly
limited in what they can do. In the language of rights introduced in the
previous chapter, each individual is said to have an entitlement right to
freedom. The vision is one in which, because individual liberty is regarded as a valuable good, it should be distributed equally among citizens in a democratic society.

Many of the leading figures in political philosophy defended different versions of a general right to liberty in the 1950s and 1960s. For example, in 1955 in a profoundly influential article on the concept of rights,
H. L. A. Hart argued that in any scheme of political morality that recog-
nizes moral rights, each individual can be said to have an equal right to be
free. This alleged right, which can be described as the general right to liberty, consists of two principal parts. The first part is the requirement of for-
bearance, which requires all others not to restrain or coerce the right-holder
except to hinder coercion or restraint. The second part is the freedom of the

right-holder to do "any action which is not one coercing or restraining or designed to injure other persons." (Hart 1984: 77)

For Hart, the general right to liberty has profound implications for the legal enforcement of morals in a democracy. (Hart 1963) At issue are laws designed to enforce the standards of behavior of the vast majority of society on sensitive issues of sexual morality such as prostitution and homosexuality. Typically, this type of law makes behavior like prostitution and homosexuality a criminal offense on the grounds that by prohibiting such behavior, the law is forcing people who might be otherwise tempted to engage in it to act morally. In other words, such laws allegedly make them better persons. In Hart's view, such laws violate an individual's equal right to liberty and, for this reason, are forbidden in a democracy.

John Rawls, in his seminal 1958 essay "Justice as Fairness," defends a general right to liberty very similar to Hart's. Rawls introduces there two principles of justice. (These principles in a revised form are defended at much greater length fifteen years later in his book *A Theory of Justice*.) The first principle says, "each person participating in a practice, or affected by it, has an equal right to the most extensive liberty compatible with a like liberty for all." (Rawls 1958: 333) His conception of justice requires that each individual is entitled to equal amounts of liberty and that this should be the greatest amount possible. Apparently, although he does not develop this point systematically, Rawls thinks this entitlement right to liberty for each individual makes sense because nobody would risk the disadvantage of having less liberty than anybody else in a process concerned with settling on principles of justice.

Consider the practice of slavery. Most people intuitively regard slavery as always unjust. For Rawls, the strength of a theory of justice that includes a principled commitment to the general right to liberty is that it is able to explain this intuition. Rawls shows that slavery necessarily involves an unequal distribution of liberty among different people and that a general right to liberty forbids such an unequal distribution. (Rawls 1958: 346)

Something like a general right to liberty is also defended by Frederick Hayek in his 1960 book *The Constitution of Liberty*. For Hayek, liberty is ". . . that condition of men in which coercion of some by others is reduced as much as is possible in society." (Hayek 1960: 11) The value of liberty derives from the fact that good consequences flow from individuals enjoying freedom. As Hayek expresses it, "the case for individual freedom rests chiefly on the recognition of the inevitable ignorance of all of us concerning a great many factors on which the achievement of our ends and welfare depends. . . . Liberty is essential in order to leave room

for the unforeseeable and unpredictable; we want it because we have
learned to expect from it the opportunity of realizing many of our aims."
(Hayek 1960: 29) While Hayek does not explicitly formulate his defense
of individual liberty in terms of rights, his account of a legal system that
respects liberty is readily amenable to the notion of a general right to liberty. In particular, Hayek maintains that "general and equal laws provide the most effective infringement against individual liberty." (Hayek
1960: 210) The upshot is that each individual ought to have an equal
right to be free.

   For Hayek, such a right has important implications for what even a
democratic state can do. Common welfare-state measures such as providing pensions through social security laws threaten the freedom of individuals because they depend on coercion. In Hayek's view, the scope
of state action should be kept to a minimum, since anything more extensive would involve the use of coercion in ways that infringe on individual liberty. (Hayek 1960: chs. 17–24)

§3   NEGATIVE AND POSITIVE FREEDOM

We have just seen that the dominant paradigm for thinking about the relation between individual liberty and democracy involves the claim that
each individual has a general right to liberty. This notion of an entitlement right to equal liberty, which has its origins in the work of John Stuart Mill, was explicitly adopted by numerous political philosophers in
the 1950s and 1960s. Two of the most important debates over individual
liberty in modern political philosophy can be properly understood only
when viewed as disputes about aspects of the claim that individuals
have a general right to liberty. The first debate is over negative and positive liberty, and the second is over the alleged priority of liberty. These
two debates are discussed in turn.

   The single most important and influential analysis of freedom by a
modern political philosopher is provided by Isaiah Berlin in his 1958
essay "Two Concepts of Liberty." Berlin in that essay distinguishes
between *negative* and *positive* liberty. These two notions of liberty share a
common thesis, namely, the belief that, "to coerce a man is to deprive
him of his freedom." (Berlin 1969: 121) The issue between the two
notions is determining exactly when a person is free. A defender of negative freedom argues that freedom is "simply the area within which a
man can act unobstructed by others." (Berlin 1969: 122) What makes this
a "negative" concept of liberty is the fact that freedom requires the absence of something. It follows on the negative concept of liberty that the

more areas in which a person can act unobstructed by others, the freer the person is. As Berlin puts it, "The extent of a man's negative liberty is, as it were, a function of what doors and how many, are open to him; upon what prospects they open; and how open they are." (Berlin 1969: xlviii) Whether or not an individual actually goes through these doors is irrelevant to whether or not he or she is free to do so. Freedom, in this sense, "is the opportunity for action, not action itself." (Berlin 1969: xlii)

The positive concept of liberty, in contrast, centers on the issue of who controls what a person does. It says that a person is truly free only when the person controls what she or he does. You enjoy positive freedom only when you are your own master. (Berlin 1969: 131) Hence, on the positive concept of liberty, the reason why coercing an individual diminishes his or her freedom is that it is someone other than that individual who is controlling what the individual does. What makes this a "positive" notion of freedom is that it requires the presence of something, e.g., self-mastery, as opposed to the absence of something, e.g., noninterference.

The main theme of Berlin's essay is that in democratic politics, the negative concept of liberty is the more valuable and insightful one. In effect, his thesis is that when it comes to the exercise of state power, we should be more concerned with identifying areas of noninterference than with who is exercising state power. This thesis is designed explicitly by Berlin to support the idea that a general right to liberty should be paramount in a democracy. Recall from the previous section that Mill claimed that the principal freedom at risk in a democracy is what he described as "individual independence." Berlin's argument, in my view, is so important and pivotal because it seeks to substantiate this claim of Mill's for modern political philosophers.

Although Berlin's discussion is complex and has many different strands, his defense of the importance of protecting negative liberty in a democracy involves two principal insights. The first insight is Berlin's observation that it is conceivable that an individual could have less negative freedom in a democracy than in, for example, a state run by hereditary leaders. (Berlin 1969: 129) His point is that in an autocratic state, there may be all sorts of aspects of an individual's life with which the government does not interfere. Conversely, a democratic state may interfere in practically all of the aspects of an individual's life. In other words, democracy in comparison with other forms of government is not special in its respect for negative liberty.

The second insight Berlin offers is that the commonly assumed link between positive freedom and democracy is also doubtful. (Berlin 1969: 145–154) We saw above that the positive concept of liberty stresses the importance of an individual being his or her own master. For many, democracy seems a logical extension of positive liberty, since in democracies people rule themselves. However, as Berlin stresses, such an extension is trickier than it first appears. Democratic governments make collective decisions that are binding on everyone, regardless of whether or not a person individually supported the decision. Suppose that you are a citizen in a democracy and that you are among those individuals who did not support a particular decision. How can you then be said to be your own master? It seems, therefore, that democracies (like all other forms of government) are compatible with positive freedom only if by being forced to comply with its collective decisions, you can still be said to be your own master. Berlin examines various attempts to explain this difficulty and concludes that all are necessarily flawed.

Berlin's essay on liberty has been subject to an immense amount of critical scrutiny, much of which is based on misinterpretations of his argument. For instance, a standard critique is that Berlin mistakenly contrasts negative and positive liberty because he fails to appreciate that each is a distinct component in a single unified concept of freedom. (MacCallum 1972; Feinberg 1973: 9–11) Perhaps the most influential statement of this critique is made by Gerald MacCallum. According to MacCallum, "freedom is ... always *of* something (an agent or agents), *from* something, *to* do, not do, become, or not become something; it is a triadic relation. (MacCallum 1972: 176) Hence, freedom involves three variables that can be expressed in the following format: "x is (is not) free from y to do (not do, become, not become) z." According to MacCallum, proponents of negative liberty like Berlin neglect the importance of the z variable. Proponents of positive liberty seemingly neglect the importance of the y variable. What is doubtful, however, is that all senses of freedom can be captured by a single concept of freedom. (Gray and Pelczynski 1984: 325–329) For example, MacCallum's triadic approach seems to overlook the idea of freedom as a status which is evident in the common contrast between a slave and a "free" man. Berlin, unlike many of his critics, seems to recognize the difficulty of settling on a single definition of freedom. More to the point, however, is that critiques like MacCallum's miss the political significance of Berlin's defense of a general right to liberty.

In my view, the most powerful criticism of Berlin's subtle defense of a general right to liberty has been made by political theorists inspired by the so-called republican, or civic humanist, tradition in the history of political thought, especially Quentin Skinner. (Skinner 1984; 1986) This criticism has its origins in the suspicion that although Berlin is right to be concerned with negative liberty, he overlooks the degree to which the preservation of negative liberty is a fragile social achievement. This suspicion has been important in many of the critiques of Berlin. (See especially Taylor 1985: ch. 8) The distinctive aspect of Skinner's critique is his observation that Berlin neglects the extent to which positive freedom—self-mastery in politics— is necessary to sustain negative liberty. Skinner concedes to Berlin (and Mill) that negative freedom—areas of noninterference by others—is the fundamental political liberty. However, he thinks that this emphasis on the importance of negative liberty generates in turn a concern for positive freedom. As Skinner puts it, "if we wish to maximize our own individual liberty, we must cease to put our trust in princes, and instead take charge of the public arena ourselves." (Skinner 1986: 249) The logic is that although negative liberty may indeed be at risk in a democracy, it is only in a democracy with politically active citizens that a secure general right to liberty is even possible.

Recently, more and more political philosophers have adopted the perspective Skinner defends about the importance of positive liberty to negative liberty and the general right to liberty. (Galston 1991; Sandel 1996a; 1996b) Although these philosophers often attack the dominance of the language of rights, this perspective can be captured in the rights discourse outlined in the previous chapter. The fundamental claim is that because individual negative liberty is a fragile social good, an entitlement right to liberty requires also that an individual have a robust set of democratic rights and that the individual exercise those rights to protect and promote his or her entitlement to negative liberty.

§4   THE PRIORITY OF LIBERTY DEBATE

We have just seen how the debate over negative and positive liberty is best situated in the context of Berlin defending one aspect of the notion that individuals have a general right to liberty. We now turn to the debate over the alleged priority of liberty.

At the center of this debate is the theory of justice defended by John Rawls in his 1971 book *A Theory of Justice*. Recall from §5 of the previous chapter that Rawls's theory involves two basic principles of justice. The first principle (which I shall call the equal liberty principle) says, "Each person is to have an equal right to the most extensive system of equal basic liberties compatible with a similar system of liberty for all." (Rawls 1971: 302) The second principle (which I shall call the equality principle) defines when social and economic inequalities are justified.

For Rawls, it is fundamental that the first principle—the equal liberty principle—have what he calls "lexical priority" over the second principle—the equality principle. By this, he means that in the setup of a just society, it is necessary first to ensure that the requirements of the equal liberty principle are met; only after this first principle has been met is it justified to consider social and economic inequalities. (Rawls 1971: 244) To put it another way, less liberty for some people and more liberty for others cannot be justified on the grounds that by having less liberty, those people benefit socially and economically. Less liberty for some cannot be justified also because it serves the common good or general welfare. As Rawls says, "liberty can be restricted only for the sake of liberty." (Rawls 1971: 250)

Rawls is claiming, then, that individual liberty or freedom has priority over all other values—equality of opportunity, general welfare, community, family values—in a just society. This insistence on the priority of liberty has significant practical implications. Consider, for example, a common justification for the system of apartheid in South Africa in the 1980s. Apartheid meant that black South Africans had considerably less freedom than their white counterparts. Apologists for apartheid often stressed the (alleged) economic benefits for blacks living in South Africa. In comparison with blacks in the rest of southern Africa, blacks in apartheid South Africa had quite a high standard of living. Thus, although sacrificing some of their equal liberty under apartheid, black South Africans enjoyed significant economic gains. Hence, these apologists argued that apartheid is not necessarily unjust because it involves a trade-off between two important values, liberty and economic well-being. Rawls's insistence on the priority of liberty provides clear grounds for rejecting such an attempt to rationalize apartheid.

The priority Rawls places on liberty distinguishes him from many of his contemporaries. For example, although Isaiah Berlin, as we have seen, defends the importance of negative liberty, he is careful to insist that liberty does not always have priority over other values like equality and the common good. (Berlin 1980: 97–102) Berlin argues that instead of always giving liberty priority, we need to be sensitive to the complexities of individual cases and weigh competing values in light of the particular circumstances.

There are, then, two distinct issues about the priority of liberty. One issue is why Rawls in *A Theory of Justice* found it necessary even to address the priority question. Certainly, one reason is for clarity and theoretical elegance. (Wolff 1977: ch. 1) Another reason is that Rawls recognized the relevance of the priority issue to the broader debates around the general right to liberty. (In his original formulation of the first principle in 1958, in his article "Justice as Fairness," Rawls did not raise the priority of liberty question.) The previous chapter emphasized that an important development in modern political philosophy was the recognition that rights function to identity forms of inequalities that are hard to justify; taking rights seriously means giving them priority. It follows, then, that a successful defense of a general right to liberty must insist, as Rawls does, on the priority of liberty.

The other issue is how exactly Rawls justifies giving liberty priority over other goods. In *A Theory of Justice*, Rawls provides two distinct justifications for the priority of liberty. The first rests, in effect, on the claim that in a society where people live by a diversity of religious and moral doctrines, without the priority of liberty some people face persecution for their particular religious or moral views by the majority. Rawls maintains that nobody would want to risk facing such persecution. (Rawls 1971: 207, 543)

The second, more sophisticated justification given by Rawls for the priority of liberty involves two complex steps. The first step relies on the idea of primary goods. Primary goods are the resources a person will require to further his or her particular way of life, regardless of the exact nature of that way of life. (Rawls 1971: 62, 93) The most important primary good for an individual, according to Rawls, is self-respect or self-esteem. The primary good of self-respect has two aspects, "first of all . . . it includes a person's sense of his own value, his secure conviction that his conception of his good, his plan of life, is worth carrying out. And second, self-respect implies a confidence in one's ability, so far as it is within one's power, to fulfill one's intentions." (Rawls 1971: 440)

The second step in Rawls' defense of the priority of liberty involves the claim that individual liberty is the most fundamental social condition necessary for self-respect. As he puts it,

> The basis for self-esteem in a just society is not . . . one's income share but the publicly affirmed distribution of fundamental rights and liberties. And this distribution being equal, everyone has a similar and secure status when they meet to conduct the common affairs of the wider society. . . . When it is the position of equal citizenship that answers to the need of status, the precedence of the equal liberties becomes all the more necessary. (Rawls 1971: 544–545)

It seems to follow from this two-step argument that liberty has priority over all other goods to be distributed in a just society.

The view that liberty or freedom is of fundamental importance has been frequently expressed by philosophers in the history of political thought. The eighteenth-century philosopher Jean Jacques Rousseau, for example, famously asserted, "To renounce liberty is to renounce being a

man, to surrender the rights of humanity and even its duties."
(Rousseau 1762: 8) Nonetheless, Rawls's bold new defense of the priority of liberty was received by many modern political philosophers with
deep suspicion and was subject to harsh criticism.

One line of strong criticism is that neither of Rawls's justifications
in fact establish the priority of liberty; rather, both establish at most the
priority of certain basic liberties. (Hart 1983: 223–247; Scanlon 1975:
186–189) The first justification, based on the risk of persecution for one's
religious or moral commitments, shows only why we should give priority to freedom of religion and freedom of conscience. It does not show
why we should give priority to other controversial freedoms like sexual
orientation or drug use. Similarly, the second justification, based on the
link between self-respect and liberty, shows only that the political liberties of equal citizenship should be given priority.

Another line of criticism is that the priority Rawls gives to liberty is
arbitrary insofar as he does not also give priority to the conditions necessary for the exercise of that liberty. (Daniels 1975: 253–281; Jacobs
1993c: 382–385) Rawls distinguishes between having a liberty and the
worth of that liberty. (Rawls 1971: 204) It might be the case that someone
has the liberty to fly to Australia. However, if that person wants to buy
an airline ticket to Australia but is too poor to afford the fare, then that
liberty has little if any worth. The worth of an individual's liberty depends on the individual's having the resources to actually exercise that
liberty, if she or he wants to. Rawls argues for the priority of liberty but
not for the priority of the worth of liberty. How important can liberty be
if it has little or no worth? It would seem that if liberty is so important
that a theory of justice should give it priority, having the resources to exercise that liberty should also be given priority.

§5   FROM LIBERTY TO BASIC LIBERTIES

These criticisms of Rawls's attempt to establish the priority of liberty reflect a major shift in modern political philosophy. Previously it was
stressed that in the 1950s and 1960s, philosophers focused on the idea of
a general right to liberty. Now, the emphasis has shifted to the idea of a
set of rights to basic liberties. The main source of this revisionist shift is
the intuition that some freedoms are more important than others and
that a general right to liberty does not capture this difference.

Rawls, in response to his critics, has clearly embraced this shift. He
now insists that his first principle of justice should be understood as as-

cribing to individuals not a general right to liberty but rather rights to certain specific basic liberties, that is,

> ... freedom of thought and liberty of conscience; the political liberties and freedom of association, as well as the freedoms specified by the liberty and integrity of the person; and finally, the rights and liberties covered by the rule of law. No priority is assigned to liberty as such, as if the exercise of something called "liberty" has a preeminent value and is the main if not the sole end of political and social justice. (Rawls 1993: 291–292)

The list of basic liberties Rawls provides here are familiar and have a long historical constituency. The proposal that they should have priority is much more modest than the view that liberty in general should have priority, as a requirement of social justice. Moreover, with some modifications, the arguments for the priority of liberty given by Rawls in *A Theory of Justice* seem to establish the priority of these basic liberties. (Rawls 1993: ch. 8) Also, it is significant that Rawls is not then claiming that liberty always has priority over the worth of liberty but rather that some basic liberties have priority over the worth of liberty.

The main source of the revisionist challenge to a general right to liberty, aside from Rawls, is Ronald Dworkin. (Dworkin 1978: ch. 12) According to Dworkin, a general right to liberty is politically significant only if it means that it is wrong for the government to interfere with someone doing something even though it is in the collective interest to do so. He points out, however, that there are laws justified by the collective interest that do restrict people's freedom in this sense but obviously do not violate their rights. An example is a traffic regulation against driving the wrong way up a one-way street. Clearly, this law is justified by the collective interest and results in people not having the freedom to drive the wrong way up that street. Yet, we do not think anyone's rights are violated by such a law. If so, it follows that there cannot be a general right to liberty.

Now, Dworkin admits that his understanding of the general right to liberty could be mistaken. That right might be said to mean not that it is wrong for the government to interfere with someone doing anything even though it is in the collective interest to do so, but rather that it is wrong for the government to interfere with certain liberties even though it is in the collective interest to do so. The point, then, is that the general right to liberty is best understood to protect not liberty in general but only certain important liberties such as free speech, freedom of association, and free religious worship.

In that case, questions about the general right to liberty become quite different. What is required is some sort of criterion for distinguishing important liberties from other liberties that are not protected by the general right to liberty. An appeal to the quantity of negative liberty involved in these different liberties is clearly inadequate. This point is particularly well made by Charles Taylor. (Taylor 1985: 219) Taylor proposed a comparison between Albania and Britain in terms of freedom, limiting consideration to bans on public religious practice and traffic regulations. Albania had, until recently, a general ban on public religious worship but has few traffic lights. Modern Britain, in contrast, has many more traffic lights but no ban on public religious practice. Although traffic lights are probably much more an everyday part of most people's public lives, we are nevertheless inclined to think of Britain as respecting liberty rights more than Albania does. This example shows two things: first, that there does seem to be a commonsense distinction between those fundamental liberties we have a right to and other less important liberties that we do not have rights to, and, secondly, that the difference between these types of liberties cannot be understood in terms of the quantity of negative liberty involved.

For Dworkin, the distinction between basic and nonbasic liberties must, therefore, be grounded only on some value or interest people have other than liberty. Yet if this is true, then it does not make sense to claim that there is a general right to liberty. Instead, there is at most a general right to that value or interest which in turn grounds rights to certain freedoms—freedoms that can then be described as basic liberties.

The shift from the general right to liberty to rights to basic liberties also has an ideological basis. Earlier, in §2, it was noted that Frederick Hayek in *The Constitution of Liberty*, pointed out the tension between a general right to liberty and extensive welfare state programs like social security and Medicare that redistribute wealth from some citizens to other citizens. The most important and philosophically sophisticated statement of this view is found in Robert Nozick's book *Anarchy, State, and Utopia*:

> Individuals have rights, and there are things no person or group may do to them (without violating their rights). . . . Our main conclusions about the state are that a minimal state, limited to the narrow functions of protection against force, theft, fraud, enforcement of contracts, and so on, is justified; that any more extensive state will violate persons' rights not to be forced to do certain things, and is unjustified . . . the state may not use its coercive apparatus for the purpose of getting some people to aid others. (Nozick 1974: ix)

The argument Nozick makes is that entitlement rights to anything other than liberty will conflict with entitlement rights to liberties. Hence, assuming the priority of the latter rights, talk of any other entitlement rights is nonsense.

For those like Rawls who have a commitment to entitlement rights beyond just liberty, the obvious response to classical liberals like Hayek and libertarians like Nozick is to restrict severely which liberty rights we should have so that the scope for conflict between them and other alleged entitlement rights is significantly reduced. (Paul 1984: 376–377) The significance of the shift from a general right to liberty to a certain set of rights to basic liberties is that it allows people like Rawls to dismiss Nozick's challenge to state redistribution between citizens, while still preserving his commitment to the importance of (some) individual liberty.

§6   WHY VALUE THE BASIC LIBERTIES?

It has just been pointed out that in recent political philosophy, there has been an important shift in the debates around the place of individual liberty in a democracy from the view that individuals have a general right to liberty to the view that what matters is that individuals have rights to certain basic liberties. Rawls's difficulties with showing the priority of liberty and Dworkin's challenge to the overall cogency of a general right to liberty explain this shift. But it still remains a problem to show why we should value even basic liberties like freedom of conscience, freedom of religious worship, freedom of expression, freedom of sexual orientation, and freedom of bodily integrity.

This problem is made even more difficult in light of an important feature of all rights to basic liberties that has been stressed by many modern rights theorists. It is a distinguishing feature of rights to basic liberties that they are potentially rights to do what is morally wrong. In other words, someone may have the right to do something that is the wrong thing for that person to do. (Waldron 1982: 29–30; Jacobs 1993a: 129–135) For example, an individual may have the right not to make a donation to help aid famine victims in a developing country, even though not to do so is the morally wrong thing to do. Similarly, an individual may have the right to express views of hate or bigotry, even though this is a morally repugnant thing to do. Likewise, looking at pornography might indeed be wrong, but people may still have a right to do so.

The importance of rights to basic liberties being potentially rights to do wrong is that it suggests that the value of those rights cannot rest on their exercise, since they can be exercised in ways that are wrong. Instead, the value of those rights must lie elsewhere. The two values most prevalent in modern political philosophy are equality and personal autonomy.

The best known proponent of the view that the rights to basic liberties are based on the value of equality is Dworkin. Recall that Dworkin argues that the distinction between basic liberties and nonbasic liberties must be grounded on some value or interest other than liberty. The particular value Dworkin proposes is equality. The general moral right all individuals in a democracy can be said to have is the right to equal respect and concern. (Dworkin 1978: 272–278; 1985: 191–198) This right requires *treatment as an equal* whereby everyone receives equal consideration in the decision-making about the distribution of valuable goods in a society but everyone may not receive the same share of those goods. On Dworkin's account, the rights to basic liberties are necessary in any decision-making procedure that treats everyone as equals. The right to sexual orientation, for instance, might be defended on the grounds that this ensures that the interests of homosexuals are given equal consideration in the distribution of goods in a society in which the vast majority are heterosexual. Similarly, freedom of speech could be defended on the grounds that it is an important device for ensuring equal consideration of minority interests that might otherwise not be heard. The broader point is that for Dworkin, rights to basic liberties are fundamentally rules of procedure in which the challenge is to ensure equality.

The main difficulty I have with Dworkin's account of the rights to basic liberties is precisely that he reduces them to procedural requirements. His account of them fits very well with, and indeed is parasitic upon, the egalitarian model of fair procedural democracy that was defended in Chapter Two. However, the rights to basic liberties seem for Dworkin to be meaningless outside of that sort of democratic decision-making procedure. Yet, intuitively, basic liberties seem valuable and seem the sort of good that people should have entitlement rights to, regardless of whether or not democracy is the only type of government that has a right to rule. To put it another way, Dworkin's account of entitlement rights to basic liberties mistakenly reduces them to democratic rights; this is a conflation of the ideal of democracy and the demands of social justice. Democracy requires political equality. As argued in Chapter Three, however, while the right of a democracy to rule rests on its meeting the requirements of social justice, it is nonsense to assume that a democratic state will by definition meet these requirements. Legislative politics in a democracy allow for the possibility that a democratic government might fail to uphold those requirements of social justice not guaranteed by a constitution.

The idea that the value of the rights to basic liberties derives from their importance to personal autonomy is the more conventional and ultimately more defensible view. The idea of personal autonomy has received careful attention recently among political philosophers. (Raz 1986; Young 1986; Gerald Dworkin 1989; Waldron 1989; Frankfurt 1989; Jacobs 1993a) Although there are considerable subtle differences over the main features and scope of personal autonomy, the core of the idea in modern accounts is remarkably similar to John Stuart Mill's ideal of the sovereign individual. (Recall from §2 Mill's phrase, "Over himself, over his own body and mind, the individual is sovereign.") As Joseph Raz puts it in his important book *The Morality of Freedom*, "The ideal of personal autonomy is the vision of people controlling, to some degree, their own destiny, fashioning it through successive decisions throughout their lives. . . . It contrasts with a life of no choices, or of drifting through life without ever exercising one's capacity to choose." (Raz 1986: 369, 371) The value of rights to basic liberties, in this view, is precisely that they give people the space to make choices about their lives, including the possibility that they might make the wrong choices.

§7   CONCLUSION

This chapter has examined the idea that everyone has a general right to liberty and the responses to that idea in modern political philosophy. The debates around negative and positive liberty and the alleged priority of liberty are important for sharpening that idea. We have found, however, that there has been a decisive shift among philosophers away from the project of fashioning a place for a general right to liberty in democratic political morality towards defending a set of moral rights to basic liberties for all individuals.

SUGGESTED READINGS

1. Berlin, Isaiah, *Four Essays on Liberty* (New York, Oxford University Press, 1969). A collection that contains Berlin's "Two Concepts of Liberty," which is the single most influential article on individual liberty in modern political philosophy.
2. Miller, David, editor, *Liberty* (New York, Oxford University Press, 1991). A wide-ranging collection of some of the most influential modern essays on freedom.

3. Gray, John, and Zbigniew Pelczynski, editors, *Conceptions of Liberty in Political Philosophy* (London, Athlone Press, 1984). A book containing useful chapters on the account of liberty in the work of major historical and modern figures in political philosophy.
4. Raz, Joseph, *The Morality of Freedom* (New York, Oxford University Press, 1986). Probably the most philosophically sophisticated modern account of the relation between political freedom and personal autonomy.
5. Rawls, John, *Political Liberalism* (New York, Columbia University Press, 1993). A book that contains the author's revision and extension of the theory of justice as fairness that he defended in his seminal book *A Theory of Justice*, published in 1971.

CHAPTER SIX

Economic Equality

◆

§1   INTRODUCTION

Few ideas in modern political philosophy have received more careful attention than the idea of equality. In Chapter Two, we saw that at the core of the democratic vision is the ideal of political equality. The commitment to political equality is widespread among modern political philosophers; this fact is a reflection of the consensus around the centrality of democracy to any serious theory of political morality. As suggested in Chapter Two, much of the disagreement about the best model of democracy stems from differences about what political equality involves. This chapter focuses not on *political* equality but on economic equality. *Economic* equality is the idea that some of the economic resources and goods that are important to the lives of individual citizens, such as wealth, education, and careers, should be distributed equally among them.

It is important to distinguish the idea of economic equality from the claim that, as a matter of fact, everyone is in some respect the same. Often, in the history of philosophy, it has been thought that the idea of economic equality is a valid principle of social justice because, as a matter of fact, everyone is in some relevant respect the same. Logically, then, any successful defense of economic equality would depend on showing the factual respect in which everyone is the same. In actuality, though, it is very difficult to identify some respect in which everyone is the same; many of us seem very different in terms of skills and talents, aspirations and goals, commitments and values. Moreover, those respects in which we seem to be roughly the same, such as physiology, seem not to be especially relevant to economic equality. The point is that it is difficult to make a case for economic equality based on some claim about how everyone is the same.

Among modern political philosophers, however, the case for economic equality does not generally rest on such a factual claim. Instead, the case for some measure of economic equality is ordinarily thought to be a logical extension of the commitment to political equality presupposed by the ideal of democracy. The democratic vision holds that governments should treat all citizens as equals. This is not a factual statement about how, with respect to some aspect of their nature, all citizens are the same but rather is a normative statement about how governments should act. If the case for economic equality is based on this sort of normative statement, then it is not weakened by the difficulty of identifying some factual respect in which people are the same. Indeed, the only way to resist this type of case for economic equality is by denying the normative appeal of democracy; and, of course, few serious modern political philosophers are willing to deny the appeal to democracy; as stressed in Chapter Two, we are all democrats.

The case for economic equality based on democracy maintains that there is an important relation between political equality and citizens enjoying some measure of equality in the distribution of valuable economic resources and goods in society. One traditional way to view this relation is to say that economic inequalities threaten the preservation of political equality. Jean-Jacques Rousseau, for example, maintained that significant inequalities in wealth jeopardize political equality. Hence, he defended restrictions on inequalities in wealth. Another way to view the relation between political and distributional equality is to say that in a democracy, inequalities in the distribution of valuable economic resources and goods need to be justified. Such economic inequalities cannot be regarded as "natural." The reasoning is that under other forms of governance such as aristocracy or monarchy, economic inequalities might seem natural and not in need of justification, whereas in a democracy, there is a presumption in favor of economic equality. This is the viewpoint now prevalent in modern political philosophy.

There are important differences among political philosophers about what are acceptable justifications for economic inequalities. Some argue that inequalities can be justified only in certain very limited circumstances; others argue that the justifications for economic inequality are numerous. These differences reflect the range of ideological perspectives on distributive justice in a democracy. The purpose of this chapter is to survey these dominant ideologies in modern political philosophy.

§2 CLASSICAL LIBERALISM

Although there are deep and important ideological differences about when inequalities are justified, it is important to recognize the basic points of agreement among political philosophers about equality. One fundamental point of agreement is, as just noted, that economic inequalities have to be justified. Another is that most political philosophers agree that there are some things that should be distributed equally among citizens and that it is difficult, if not impossible, to justify inequalities with regard to these things. Chapter four explained that these things are precisely those to which individuals can be said to have entitlement rights. This sort of consensus was implicit in the previous chapter on individual liberty. The assumption made there was that whatever moral rights to freedom individuals might be said to have in a democracy, these rights should be distributed equally among all citizens. The point is that freedom is one valuable resource that can be distributed among citizens and that some of that liberty—the so-called basic liberties—should be the same for everyone.

Classical liberals emphasize that a government must be limited in what it can do. The main theme is that the most important requirements of political morality set significant limitations on how the government can treat its citizens. Classical liberalism, which is associated with major figures in the history of political thought, including John Locke, Adam Smith, and John Stuart Mill, in its most familiar form expresses the limitations on the government through a theory of individual rights. Most classical liberals stress the rights to basic liberties identified in §5 of Chapter five. Taking these rights seriously, in their view, allows only for a government significantly limited in what it can do.

For contemporary proponents of classical liberalism, the general notion of a limited government based on individual rights leads logically to a particular principle of economic equality. This principle is commonly described as formal equality of opportunity. *Formal equality of opportunity* prohibits legal barriers to the access to valuable economic resources and educational and career opportunities which are based on race, sex, religion, ethnic origin, and other physical attributes of an individual that are irrelevant to that resource or opportunity. It guarantees to individuals the freedom to enjoy the resources they want or to pursue the opportunities they desire without state interference based on their race, religion, sex, and so on. The well-known phrase, "Careers open to talents," neatly captures the essence of the principle of formal equality of opportunity. (Hayek 1982: 84) It functions, then, much like rights to liberty in the sense that it sets limitations on the sort of economic mechanism the government can use to distribute resources and opportunities. Because it limits government and therefore promotes negative liberty, this principle of economic equality fits well with the core of classical liberalism.

Formal equality of opportunity is a significant principle of political morality. It prohibits some of the political policies and practices that have often been characteristic of modern governments in the United States and elsewhere. For example, it condemns many of the racist laws that motivated the civil rights movement in the 1950s and 1960s. Similarly, it provides a basis for objecting to sexist public policies that treat men and women differently. Likewise, it would make it difficult to justify policies such as mandatory school prayer in public schools, since such laws seem to deny equality to those of different religions.

However, it is also noteworthy that classical liberals have typically thought that formal equality of opportunity dovetails well with the use of economic markets for the allocation and distribution of scarce resources. Markets set prices on resources by gathering information about the supply and demand for particular resources among individuals. Those prices determine how resources are allocated and to whom they are distributed. The standard contrast to a market-pricing mechanism based on the preferences and wants of individuals is a centralized government institution run by bureaucrats who set prices in light of their own plans for the nation's economies. In capitalist economies, markets are the preferred and prevailing mechanism for allocating and distributing resources. Classical liberals have characteristically embraced the widespread use of markets because allegedly they promote individual liberty; bureaucratic planners inevitably interfere with the lives of individual citizens by imposing their plans on them. (See, for example, Gray 1986: ch. 8) Economic markets conform to formal equality of opportunity because they involve no legal barriers based on race, sex, religion, and so on. The principal legal barrier that economic markets do impose on individuals is the ability to pay; this barrier is not, however, ordinarily thought by classical liberals to be prohibited by formal equality of opportunity.

The rationale for formal equality of opportunity is that legal barriers based on race, sex, and so on would yield unjustified economic inequalities. With no such barriers in place, any resulting economic inequalities would be justified because they would be a consequence of taking seriously the rights to basic liberties. In effect, with no discriminatory barriers to the access to economic markets, all individuals allegedly begin from an equal starting condition and are free to make the most of the opportunities that are available to them.

§3   LIBERTARIANISM

Challenging the principle of formal equality of opportunity and, hence, classical liberalism is a unifying theme among competing ideologies. For libertarians, it is significant that formal equality of opportunity not be extended beyond the requirement that prohibits legal barriers based on race, sex, religion, ethnic origins, and so on. Libertarians share with classical liberals the commitment to the notion of the limited state. However, what distinguishes libertarianism is the view that this limited state must be a minimal state—often described as a night-watchman state—restricted to enforcing contracts, preventing fraud, and protecting private property. The most sophisticated statement of libertarianism is provided by Robert Nozick. (Nozick's views were briefly outlined in §5 of the previous chapter.)

For libertarians like Nozick, individuals each have moral rights to those things they own. Those things include not only physical resources in the world like land but also their own body and the accompanying natural endowments and labor power. The moral rights of ownership or private property rights give the holder of those rights exclusive discretion over the use and transfer of the property. Every individual has some moral rights to private property because everyone is at the least the exclusive owner of himself or herself. (Nozick 1974: 172) Libertarians typically defend the importance of private property rights because those rights are allegedly closely connected to individual liberty, although this connection often relies on a confusion of private property and freedom. (Nozick 1974: ch. 3; Steiner 1994: chs. 2–3; Cohen 1981; 1986)

The most fundamental (and controversial) claim Nozick makes about equality is that economic inequalities can be justified because those inequalities can be remedied for only by violating the private property rights of individuals. His point, in other words, is that respect for moral rights to private property constitutes a justification for economic inequalities. As Nozick puts it,

> The major objection to speaking of everyone's having a right to various things such as equality of opportunity, life, and so on, and enforcing this right, is that these "rights" require a substructure of things and materials and action; and other people may have rights and entitlements over these.

... The particular rights over things fill the space of rights, leaving no room for general rights to be in a certain material condition. (Nozick 1974: 238)

Nozick makes the related point that private property rights also make it impossible to preserve economic equality, even should it be achieved without initially violating anyone's rights. (Nozick 1974: 160–164; Cohen 1991; Fried 1995) Imagine that there is economic equality in Chicago so that everyone living there, including the basketball player Michael Jordan, has $1,000 each. Presumably, each individual has the freedom to spend their $1,000 however he or she chooses. Suppose, though, that 10,000 people in Chicago would like to pay Michael Jordan $10 each to see him play for the Chicago Bulls. In that case, each of them would then have only $990, but, of course, Michael Jordan would have $101,000. This economic inequality would seem to be justified because of the private property rights each person has to spend the wealth they are entitled to, however they want.

Libertarians insist, then, that significant economic inequalities can be justified in a regime of private property rights. Classical liberals, in contrast, tend to downplay this conclusion, highlighting instead the role of freedom in justifying certain economic inequalities. The libertarian perspective depends ultimately on the validity of its account of private property rights.

§4   CONSERVATISM

Conservatism does not appeal to abstract principles to guide political decision-making. It rejects using the state to transform society radically. Instead, conservatives favor using the state only to undertake piecemeal change and reinforce the status quo. They call for the legal enforcement of public morals. (Devlin 1965) The social institutions that conservatives typically defend are the family, churches, and private property. Unlike classical liberals, conservatives do not defend these institutions primarily because they promote individual liberty but rather because these are traditional institutions in our society that have (allegedly) worked. (Oakeshott 1962: 39–40 & 168–196; Hayek 1960: Postscript)

What conservatives find lacking in the justifications for economic inequalities defended by classical liberals and libertarians is any appeal to the concept of desert. (MacIntyre 1981: ch. 17; Glazer 1988: ch. 9) Yet, traditionally the concept of desert seems to be very important for justifying inequalities. The strongest justification for someone receiving more than someone else is that she or he deserves more; there is something she or he did that is the basis for grounding this claim of desert. For example, if you work much harder than someone else, it seems clear that you deserve to have a greater material reward. For most conservatives, this idea of desert is not an abstract notion but must be situated in the distinct communities where the wealth is being distributed. Indeed, while the standards of desert may vary from community to community, it seems that all such communities must have some sort of standard of desert, and, therefore, in all communities there will be significant economic inequalities justified on desert, and not on private property rights nor individual liberty.

Classical liberals and libertarians hesitate to embrace the idea of desert because of the tension between desert, on the one hand, and private property rights and economic markets, on the other hand. The tension arises because neither private property rights nor economic markets can guarantee that the allocation and distribution of resources will result in people getting what they deserve. Both factors reward individuals as much on the basis of luck, as a matter of desert. (Hayek 1960: 93–99)

§5   EGALITARIAN LIBERALISM

Egalitarian liberals share with classical liberals the concern with the rights to basic liberties. However, they also defend much more economic equality. Unlike classical liberals, egalitarian liberals accept far fewer sorts of justifications for economic inequalities. Two of the most influential modern American political philosophers, John Rawls and Ronald Dworkin, subscribe to egalitarian liberalism. Rawls and Dworkin differ, however, over when exactly economic inequalities can be justified.

For Rawls, economic inequalities cannot be justified on the basis of the concept of desert. (Rawls 1971: 310–315) In his view, desert is far too vague and unclear to justify the degree of inequality conservatives claim. Likewise, Rawls rejects the libertarian defense of inequalities based on property rights because he does not see any basis for a system of private property like that assumed by Nozick. (Nagel 1982; Scheffler 1982) The alternative which Rawls defends is the idea that "injustice . . . is simply inequalities that are not to the benefit of all." (Rawls 1971: 62)

Rawls provides a specific formulation of this idea with his second principle of justice as fairness. (The two principles of Rawls's theory of social justice are outlined in §5 of Chapter Four and also discussed in §4 of the last chapter.) That principle states,

Social and economic inequalities are to be arranged so that they are both:
(a) to the greatest benefit of the least advantaged . . .
(b) attached to offices and positions open to all under conditions of fair equality of opportunity. (Rawls 1971: 302)

Part (a) is called the *difference principle*, part (b) the principle of *fair equality of opportunity*. It is significant that fair equality of opportunity has lexical priority over the difference principle in the sense that in a just society ensuring fair equality of opportunity is to be given consideration first, and only after this consideration will the difference principle come into play. The combination of fair equality of opportunity and the difference principle constitute what Rawls calls *democratic equality*.

Democratic equality is best explained as a reaction to the principle of formal equality of opportunity embraced by classical liberals. *Formal* equality of opportunity requires that everyone have the same legal rights of access to all advantaged social positions and offices, and that these positions and offices be open to talents in the sense that they are to be distributed to those able and willing to strive for them. For Rawls, however, this principle is deeply problematic because it discounts the initial starting positions of individuals. Similarly motivated and endowed individuals may differ in their success under formal equality of opportunity because they come from different socioeconomic and family backgrounds. Is this fair? What Rawls calls the principle of *fair* equality of opportunity is designed to address this flaw with formal equality of opportunity. It maintains that "those who are at the same level of talent and ability, and have the same willingness to use them, should have the same prospects of success regardless of their initial place in the social system, that is, irrespective of the income class into which they are born." (Rawls 1971: 73)

The reasoning Rawls gives for shifting from formal to fair equality of opportunity leads ultimately to the difference principle. The basis for objecting to legal barriers based on race, sex, religious commitments, and ethnicity under formal equality of opportunity is that such barriers would seem to be based on morally arbitrary distinctions, that is to say, there are no moral grounds for treating people differently because of their race, sex, religion, and ethnicity. Similarly, since the family which an individual is born into is merely the outcome of a "natural lottery" and hence a matter of moral luck, any attempt to justify inequalities between individuals on the basis of familial background is morally arbitrary and, therefore, misdirected. The principle of fair equality of opportunity is an improvement on the principle of formal equality of opportunity because it addresses the moral arbitrariness of family and socioeconomic background. (Rawls 1971: 72–75)

By the same logic, the particular natural endowments and talents possessed by an individual are, like family background, morally arbitrary. For Rawls, then, "There is no more reason to permit the distribution of income and wealth to be settled by the distribution of natural assets than by historical and social fortune." (Rawls 1971: 74) If economic inequalities cannot be justified by an appeal to differences in talents or family background, how then might inequalities be justified? The answer Rawls provides with the difference principle is that economic inequalities must be to the advantage of the least well-off; for any justified inequalities would then seem to make everyone better off and, therefore, make those inequalities acceptable to even those who are the least well-off.

Ronald Dworkin shares with Rawls a commitment to egalitarian liberalism. (Dworkin 1978: ch. 6; 1985: ch. 9) However, he rejects Rawls's idea that inequalities can be justified only when they are to the advantage of the least well-off. For Dworkin, the difference principle is misconceived because it allows for only one possible justification for economic inequality, namely, that the inequality benefits the least well-off. (Dworkin 1981: 343) In his view, economic inequalities between individuals can be justified also because of differences in ambition, taste, and occupation. To illustrate, imagine that one individual is ambitious and works very hard, while another individual is lazy; some economic inequalities between these two individuals would seem to be justified because of differences in their ambitions.

The fundamental distinction Dworkin makes is between economic inequalities that are a function of an individual's circumstances and economic inequalities that are a function of an individual's choices. (Dworkin 1981: 302; 1987: 18–19; 1991: 36–38; Cohen 1989: 921–924; Kymlicka 1990: ch. 3) An individual's circumstances are those features of an individual that are not within the domain of his or her choices. Race, sex, physical and mental disabilities, and ethnicity are all examples of an individual's circumstances. For Dworkin, inequalities that are a function of an individual's circumstances cannot be justified. In contrast, inequalities that are a function of his or her choices such as, for example, inequalities that can be traced to differences in ambitions, views about what constitutes a valuable life, tastes, and personal preferences, are justified. The rationale Dworkin gives for this distinction is that whereas inequalities that are a function of an individual's circumstances are a matter of luck, inequalities that are a function of an individual's choices are not. Egalitarian liberals object to economic inequalities that are a matter of luck. Although Dworkin then shares with Rawls the view that

classical liberals, libertarians, and conservatives are mistaken about
when economic inequalities are justified, his reason is not that they fail
to give priority to the worst-off but rather that they allow for justified
economic inequalities that derive from the luck of an individual's circumstances.

§6   FEMINISM

Recent feminism has made an invaluable contribution to the debate in
modern political philosophy over economic equality. A major theme is
that liberals, conservatives, socialists, and Marxists have all traditionally
assumed that many of the economic inequalities between men and
women are justified; most modern political philosophers have focused
on *inequalities between families* and their effect on the opportunities of individuals. This fact is evident, for example, in Rawls's argument for fair
equality of opportunity over formal equality of opportunity. He emphasized, as we saw above, that different family backgrounds significantly
affect the initial starting position of individuals in a competition for
scarce opportunities and resources in a society. For feminists, however,
it is significant that the opportunities of women are also affected in a
major way by *inequalities within families*. (Hartmann 1981; Okin 1987;
1989: ch. 7; Rhode 1989: ch. 7)

The fact that the opportunities of women are affected by inequalities within families has become very apparent in the United States because of the increase in family breakdowns. The evidence based on
analyses of these family breakdowns shows that women and children
suffer significant decreases in their material standard of living while
men enjoy an increase. (Weitzman 1986; Okin 1991) Much of the inequality within the family stems from an unequal distribution of domes-
tic labor and child care. Women typically choose to give up their jobs
and careers in order to have and take care of children. The consequence
is that in many families, the man is the principal breadwinner, and, if
the family breaks down, the woman does not have employment that
supports a standard of living comparable to when the husband and wife
pooled incomes. For feminists, a defensible theory of economic equality
must be able to explain why such economic inequalities are unjustified.

For classical liberals and libertarians, however, economic inequalities of this sort between men and women are justified because they can
be remedied only by violating the freedom and property rights of men.
Likewise, for an egalitarian liberal like Dworkin, these economic in-

equalities would seem to be justified because they are a function of the choices women make about their lives.

Some feminists have argued at length that John Rawls's idea of democratic equality can be extended to address economic inequalities that are a consequence of injustices within the family. (Okin 1989: chs. 1, 4, 8) Fair equality of opportunity raises the issue of whether, after divorce, men and women start from different initial positions and, therefore, whether women are unfairly disadvantaged. (Jacobs 1994) Moreover, the difference principle requires that economic inequalities between men and women must be to the benefit of women in order to be justified. Since it is doubtful that existing inequalities meet this requirement, the difference principle would support the view of feminists that such inequalities cannot be justified.

Others argue that feminists need to develop their own theories of equality that are distinct from traditional ideological perspectives like liberalism and Marxism. All of these perspectives are dominated by a male perspective on inequality. For some, this male perspective reduces inequality to questions of rights. A different feminist perspective would be to treat economic inequality as a problem of showing compassion for the disadvantaged and caring for others. (Gilligan 1982; Larabee 1993) Others have argued, however, that the problem is not so much with the rights paradigm but with the fact that in most instances the assumption made is that the bearer of the right is a man. (MacKinnon 1987: ch. 2; 1989) What we need on this view is an account of gender equality that transcends the current male-dominated standards for judging economic injustices. Although these alternative feminist perspectives have provided insight into some areas of public policy such as sexual harassment and violence against women, they have yet to prove fruitful in the debates in political philosophy over economic equality.

§7   MARKET SOCIALISM

Although the idea of market socialism is not an especially new one, among political philosophers it has recently emerged as a very influential political ideology. Market socialism is ordinarily contrasted to state socialism, which was the form of socialism that prevailed in the former Soviet Union and much of Eastern Europe. (Miller 1989: 5–11) Both forms of socialism reject the extensive private ownership of the means of production—factories, land, technology, industrial equipment, and so on—characteristic of a capitalist economy. State socialism requires that the ownership of the means of production be in the hands of the state.

The state, through its bureaucrats, then makes decisions about how and what is to be produced in the nation's economy. Market socialism, in contrast, socializes the means of production not by putting the ownership in the hands of the state but rather by providing the workers who labor in the factories with collective ownership over their factories. Firms in market socialism would not be owned by capitalists nor by the state but rather by the workers as a group. The consequence is that decisions about the economy are made cooperatively by groups of workers at these factories. Economic markets are, then, necessary to coordinate these decisions in much the same way that classical liberalism prescribes. (See §2 preceding.)

Market socialism is now defended by both Marxists and non-Marxist socialists. Marxism will be discussed in the next section of this chapter. Here, the focus is on non-Marxist proponents of market socialism. Non-Marxist socialists have ordinarily highlighted the importance of distributional equality, and most such socialists traditionally objected to exclusive reliance on economic markets because they create economic inequalities. (Tawney 1964; Cole 1975; Crosland 1957) For those who defend market socialism, it is, then, necessary to justify the economic inequalities that result from the reliance on markets.

How philosophers respond depends on what led them to market socialism. There are two positions that are especially prevalent. For some, workers controlling factories is a logical extension of political democracy. Market socialism on this view is a form of economic democracy in the sense that it is workers ruling over themselves in the workplace. As Robert Dahl puts it, "*If* democracy is justified in governing the state, then it must *also* be justified in governing economic enterprises; and to say that it is *not* justified in governing economic enterprises is to imply that it is not justified in governing the state." (Dahl 1985: 110) The only economic inequalities that are not justified are those that threaten economic democracy.

The other position market socialists sometimes take in attempting to justify the economic inequalities of a market economy is surprisingly similar to the justification for economic inequalities emphasized by conservatives. Recall that conservatives stress the importance of the concept of desert in justifications of economic inequalities. Some market socialists likewise argue that the economic inequalities that would exist under market socialism are deserved. For example, David Miller in his book *Market, State, and Community: Theoretical Foundations of Market Socialism*, argues that desert is the core value in a theory of distributive justice and that we need a public standard to measure desert. His defense of economic markets is precisely that they provide this standard. The upshot, then, is that any economic inequalities resulting from markets can be said to be deserved. (Miller 1989: ch. 6)

This conclusion warrants two comments. The first is that although classical liberals and libertarians are perhaps the strongest proponents of capitalism and economic markets, neither defend markets for the reason that they track what people deserve. Instead, they defend markets because markets promote freedom or respect private property; they tend to be skeptical about linking markets to ideas of desert. Ironically, then, socialists like Miller are making even stronger normative claims about economic markets than are classical liberals and libertarians. The second comment is about the concept of desert. Most modern political philosophers acknowledge that our standards of desert are very complex and that, as a consequence, it is difficult to use them to justify particular instances of economic inequality. As Michael Walzer explains, "Desert is a strong claim, but it calls for difficult judgments; and only under very special conditions does it yield specific distributions." (Walzer 1983: 25) The point is that the claim that markets track desert not only runs contrary to traditional defenses of market economies, but also strains the notion of desert.

§8   EGALITARIAN MARXISM

Among Marxist political philosophers, one of the central recent debates has been around whether Karl Marx and subsequent Marxists are committed to an egalitarian vision of social justice in which economic equality is a normative ideal to be pursued and fought for. The intuition most people have is that of course Marx and Marxism are committed to equality. However, it is notable that Marx himself in his volumes and volumes of writings provides no explicit and unqualified endorsement of economic equality. Some philosophers have argued that Marx's critique of capitalism does not depend on a commitment to equality because it is based not on a moral theory of rights or social justice but rather on a scientific analysis of society and human history. Moreover, Marx was suspicious of and ultimately rejected the idea of equality because, in his view, it was used in practice to justify class oppression. (Wood 1986) Others have argued that Marx's social and political theory relies on the moral principle of economic equality, even though Marx himself seems not to have realized this. For them, it is not possible to make sense of Marxism without a commitment to economic equality. (Elster 1985: ch. 4.3; Geras 1989; Peffer 1990: ch. 4) The view that Marxism involves this commitment to equality I call egalitarian Marxism. It now prevails among moral and political philosophers committed to Marxism.

Egalitarian Marxism, like other ideological perspectives within the domain of the democratic vision of politics, must face the issue of when economic inequalities are justified. Many egalitarian Marxists now embrace the general approach to justifying inequality taken by John Rawls. (Cohen 1989; 1991; Peffer 1990: chs. 9–10; Van Parijs 1992: 467–470; Roemer 1992: 450–451 and 462–464; 1994: §1) Recall from our discussion of egalitarian liberalism in §5 that Rawls's difference principle says that economic and social inequalities are justified only when they are to the benefit of the worst-off in society. The rationale that underlies the difference principle is that if certain inequalities make the worst-off in society better off, then it follows that these inequalities are justified because everyone is better off as a consequence of them. Hence, as many egalitarian Marxists concede, it would be irrational to deny that such inequalities are justified because that would amount to saying it is better to have less than more.

What then distinguishes egalitarian Marxists from egalitarian liberals? The most cogent response provided by egalitarian Marxists revolves around the justification of economic incentives. For classical liberals like Hayek and egalitarian liberals like Rawls, it is generally assumed that in a market economy some significant inequalities in income are necessary to provide economic incentives for people to work hard and direct their skills and talents in ways that are valuable for society. To illustrate, consider the case of being a surgeon, a career which is socially valuable but generally requires a lot of training and involves both intelligence and intensive effort. In market economies, surgeons are paid high incomes; the logic is that a high income provides talented individuals with an economic incentive to pursue surgery as a career. Of course, we are all better off by having such individuals as surgeons. In other words, the economic inequalities that result from providing those economic incentives conform to Rawls's difference principle and, therefore, are justified because they benefit even the worst-off in society.

Egalitarian Marxists, unlike egalitarian liberals, question the normative claim that inequalities stemming from economic incentives are justified. They ordinarily concede that pretax wage differentials may be necessary for economic markets to operate properly by, for example, paying surgeons more than waiters in order to signal to talented individuals that they should become surgeons rather than waiters because surgeons are socially more valuable. However, in their view, this is no reason not to use an income tax system to tax the income of the surgeon so that in the end there is very little difference between what the waiter and the surgeon have in (after-tax) disposable income to spend on things that the individual values. (Roemer 1992: 462-463)

Egalitarian Marxists have argued that economic incentives are in fact inconsistent with the general spirit of the difference principle. Gerald Cohen argues that although Rawls presents the difference principle so that it allows for inequalities that are necessary for economic incentives, that presentation is inconsistent with the general idea of community which underlies the difference principle. (Cohen 1992: 310–327) That idea emphasizes the importance of social cooperation and the view that although people contribute with an eye to what they receive and would not contribute unless they received something in return, they do not contribute because they receive something in return; they contribute because of their shared sense of community fellowship with other members of their society. The upshot of Cohen's analysis is that for the sake of consistency, egalitarian liberals like Rawls should give up his view that inequalities created by the necessity of economic incentives for individuals are consistent with the requirements of an egalitarian theory of social justice.

§9 POSTMODERNISM

The perspective of postmodernism has become immensely influential among political philosophers in recent years. What characterizes postmodernists is a deep-rooted skepticism about an enduring simple truth in politics. They reject the concern of modernity with the discovery of single unified truths about human nature, justice, religion, and so on. Although this skepticism takes many forms, it is generally motivated by the view that what is missing in the dominant ideological perspectives of the twentieth century—liberalism, conservatism, Marxism, socialism—is sensitivity to the extent to which claims about truth and knowledge function in politics as an exercise of power by some groups in society over other groups. The modern quest for truth results in those groups who hold beliefs that differ from the "truth" being marginalized and subject to domination. For example, claims about Western religious beliefs typically are exclusive and assume that only one view can be true; religious practices that are different such as those often practiced by members of non-Western ethnic groups are represented as barbaric and uncivilized. Postmodernists emphasize that the marginality and disadvantage experienced by members of these groups is a direct consequence of the assumption that there is a single objective truth about religious beliefs. If we reject that assumption, it no longer is plausible to represent such groups as barbaric and uncivilized. (Rorty 1985; 1989: ch. 4; Minnow 1990)

There is in postmodernist political philosophy very little explicit effort to explain when economic inequalities are justified. A major postmodernist theme is, however, that much of the discussion in modern political philosophy of economic inequality is misconceived for two related reasons. The first reason is that many political philosophers lose sight of the fact that what is primary in discussions of economic equality is not the possession of some object but rather a relationship between persons. (Young 1990a: 25–26; Minnow & Shanley 1996: 4–29) Often, for example, rights to economic equality—what I have called entitlement rights—are talked about as if they are rights to things, whereas defenders of postmodernism insist that such rights are best thought of as relational. As Iris Young explains, "Rights are not fruitfully conceived as possessions. Rights are relationships, not things; they are institutionally defined rules specifying what people can do in relation to one another. Rights refer to doing more than having, to social relationships that enable or constrain action." (Young 1990a: 25) The upshot of this emphasis is that when thinking about justifications for economic inequalities, political philosophers should focus on relationships of inequality between persons.

The second related respect in which, according to postmodernism, much modern political philosophy is misconceived in its approach to distributive justice is the way in which the existence of a particular economic inequality is taken as a given. What postmodernist analysis emphasizes is that what counts as an economic inequality is itself a matter of language, culture, and specific discourses within a society. What counts as a need, for instance, is not something that can be assumed but is rather a matter of cultural interpretation. Philosophers seriously concerned with distributive justice should, then, shift their focus to discourses about needs. As Nancy Fraser explains, "Usually, the politics of needs is understood to concern the distribution of satisfactions [of needs]. In my approach, by contrast, the focus is the *politics of need interpretation*." (Fraser 1989: 292)

The implication of this postmodernist critique of existing approaches to economic equality is that concerns about economic inequalities are indistinguishable from cultural inequalities. Since the latter sort of inequalities are always particular to specific circumstances and since there are no universal principles for addressing cultural inequalities, likewise it must be the case for the postmodernist that there is no single or universal response to the question of when economic inequalities are justified.

§10 CONCLUSION

This chapter has surveyed eight different competing ideological perspectives on economic inequality. The theme that unifies the discussion is the assumption across these perspectives that economic inequalities must be justified, and that such inequalities cannot be assumed by political philosophers to be "natural." This preoccupation with providing normative foundations for economic inequalities distinguishes the discussion of distributive justice in modern philosophy from practically all of the political philosophy that preceded it.

The fact that there are such deep ideological differences about when economic inequalities are justified is an important dimension of the democratic vision of politics. Competing political parties and elected officials adopt different ideological stances about economic equality that are reflected in the policy-making procedure. Perhaps the most divisive and important realm of policy-making for the legislature in a democracy is precisely around how and when to address economic inequalities. The prominence of this aspect of politics in the democratic vision distinguishes it from both the theory and the practice of earlier epochs in politics. As Richard Tawney insightfully pointed out fifty years ago in his landmark book *Equality,*

> Seen in historical perspective, the attempt to combine the equality of civil and political rights, which is of the essence of democracy, with the inequality of economic and social opportunities, which is of the essence of capitalism, is still in its first youth. There is sufficient experience, however, to suggest that the result represents, at best, a transitional arrangement. As the mass of the population becomes conscious of the powers which democracy confers, they naturally use them to press their demands. In proportion as they use them, democracy itself wears a different, and less innocuous, guise in the eyes of classes who formerly regarded it with indifference. (Tawney 1964: 1938 Preface)

SUGGESTED READINGS

1. Rawls, John, *A Theory of Justice* (Cambridge, Harvard University Press, 1971). The most influential book in modern political philosophy.
2. Arthur, John, and William Shaw, editors, *Justice and Economic Distribution, Second Edition.* (Englewood Cliffs, NJ, Prentice-Hall, 1991). A wide-ranging collection of articles on distributive justice.

3. Roemer, John, editor, *Analytical Marxism* (New York, Cambridge University Press, 1986). A collection of articles that is an excellent pulse on recent work in Marxism on distributive justice.

4. Walzer, Michael, *Spheres of Justice* (New York, Basic Books, 1983). An influential account of social justice that emphasizes the value of using a plurality of standards for assessing inequality.

5. Young, Iris Marion, *Justice and the Politics of Difference* (Princeton, Princeton University Press, 1990). A book with a very accessible and well-defended statement of one postmodernist perspective on social justice.

CHAPTER SEVEN
Democratic Community

———————◆———————

§1   INTRODUCTION

Theories of social justice have traditionally accounted for three principal values: liberty, equality, and community. (In the history of political thought, the latter often was called "fraternity;" most modern political philosophers now use the gender-neutral language of community.) During much of the twentieth century, however, political philosophers have concentrated mainly on the values of liberty and equality to the detriment of the value of community. The preoccupation of political philosophy with liberty and equality is evident, for example, in John Rawls's formulation of his theory of justice as fairness. Rawls defends, as we saw in preceding chapters, two principles of justice, one that addresses the distribution of freedom and the second that addresses social and economic inequalities. He does not include a principle of justice that explicitly addresses the value of community. The neglect of the value of community in modern theories of justice has emerged as one of the most influential themes in recent moral and political philosophy. This chapter addresses the importance of this renewed interest in the value of community to the democratic vision of politics.

§2   THE SIGNIFICANCE OF COMMUNITY

What is community? For our purposes, a community can be understood as an association of people who share some values and a history, participate in certain common activities, and have a strong bond of solidarity

to each other. (Phillips 1993: 14–18) It is also characteristic of a community that the interests of individuals are conceived of not as independent
of the community but rather as bound up with the community. As
Buchanan explains, "Each member thinks of furthering the community's
ends as a gain for *us*, not as a gain for herself which happens to be ac-
companied by similar gains for other individuals constituting the
group." (Buchanan 1989: 857) Examples of typical communities are
church congregations, extended families, grass roots political organizations, fraternities and sororities, and unions.

All citizens of democratic states are also members of their own particular communities. These communities are more often than not integral to who we are. They provide us with our personal identity. As Alasdair MacIntyre explains, "I am someone's son or daughter, someone
else's cousin or uncle; I am a citizen of this or that city, a member of this
or that guild or profession; I belong to this clan, that tribe, this nation.
. . . As such, I inherit from the past of my family, my city, my tribe, my
nation, a variety of debts, inheritances, rightful expectations and obligations. These constitute the given of my life." (MacIntyre 1981: 204-205)

The observation that membership in particular communities is fundamental to our personal identity is largely an empirical claim and can
generally be confirmed through anecdotal reflection. Most of us accept
that, as MacIntyre points out, who we are is a function in part of the various communities to which we belong. What is the significance of this
observation to the democratic vision of politics? What are its implications for a theory of social justice?

Presumably, it suggests that our membership in particular communities and hence the existence of those communities is very important to
individual well-being. Without those communities, our personal identity would seem to disintegrate; we would not have a sense of who we
are. An account of social justice should, then, make the protection and
promotion of community a pressing concern. The practical question is
which communities should be protected and promoted in a democracy.

§3   THE COMMUNITARIAN CHALLENGE
TO THE PRIMACY OF RIGHTS

Communitarianism is the view that the value and significance of community has been neglected in the theory and practice of politics and
should be taken more seriously by political philosophers. (Gutmann
1985) Communitarianism has been a constant and reoccurring theme
among both radicals and conservatives in the history of political

thought. (Walzer 1990: 6–7; Phillips 1993: 3) Karl Marx and Frederick Engels in the *Communist Manifesto of 1848* warned, for example, that traditional communities would degenerate as capitalism spreads so that, in their words, "all that is solid melts into air." Similarly, Edmund Burke in his famous reactionary attack on the French Revolution of 1789 lamented about how the traditional community institutions of civility and religion were disintegrating in France. Among modern political philosophers, communitarianism has once again reemerged as an important theme.

The modern revival of communitarianism in political philosophy has been influenced by the widespread perception that traditional forms of community like the family, churches, neighborhoods, and schools in the United States and elsewhere are under siege. (Bellah et. al., 1985) This conclusion is based on sensitivity to the dramatic increase in divorces and family breakdown, the growth of illegitimate births, the spread of unorthodox religions, escalating crime, increasing drug use, and the upsurge in illiteracy among youth. For some communitarians, the breakdown of community is imminent and needs to be addressed immediately. Their view is that while the situation is indeed grave, it is still possible to be optimistic about the future of the traditional forms of community. As Michael Sandel puts it, "our most pressing moral and political project is to revitalize those civic republican possibilities implicit in our tradition but fading in our time." (Sandel 1984: 249) Other communitarians are much more pessimistic, maintaining, in effect, that traditional forms of community are already dead. MacIntyre says, "What matters at this stage is the construction of local forms of community within which civility and the intellectual and moral life can be sustained through the new dark ages which are already upon us. . . . the barbarians are not waiting beyond the frontiers; they have already been governing us for quite some time. And it is our lack of consciousness of this that constitutes part of our predicament." (MacIntyre 1981: 245)

For American political scientists and sociologists, an important task has been to link the alleged decline in traditional forms of community to social and political institutions. The logic is that if the source of the decline is a certain institution or policy, then this decline can be reversed by reforming or abolishing the institution or policy in question. A common focal point is American social policy. The conservative policy analyst Charles Murray argued at length in his 1984 book, *Losing Ground*, that welfare reforms since the early 1960s are the major cause of the breakdown of the traditional family because they encourage dependency on the state, reward illegitimacy, and undermine the work ethic. (Murray 1984) The liberal policy analyst Mickey Kaus traces the decline of traditional forms of community in his 1992 book, *The End of Equality*, to the insistence in social policy reform in the 1960s, 1970s, and 1980s on addressing inequalities in income, rather than inequalities in social status. (Kaus 1992)

For communitarian political philosophers, however, the threat to community comes not just from political practice; it is also a reflection of deep flaws in the dominant perspectives in political philosophy. The communitarian critique has numerous strands and operates at many different levels. (See, for example, Kymlicka 1988; Holmes 1989; Mulhall & Swift 1992: 35–164) Some of these are at the level of metaethics and question whether it makes sense to talk about objective moral principles. Another frequent communitarian theme is criticism of the philosophical psychology that prevails in behaviorism and cognitive science. Yet another strand of critique is directed at prevailing schools of thought in philosophy of language. Indeed, it can be pointed out with some irony that communitarianism is associated with so many controversial philosophical claims that the philosophers most often identified as communitarian question that identification. (Bell 1993: 4)

The most important and relevant dimension of the communitarian critique to our discussion of the democratic vision of politics is the challenge to the primacy of rights and the priority of meeting the requirements of justice in democratic politics. (See also, for example, Buchanan 1989: 855–856.) In the previous three chapters on social justice, the language I used was predominantly the language of individual rights. Rights, as I explained in Chapter Four, set side constraints on what governments can do; individual rights allow the interests of individuals to trump government decisions that look to what serves the general welfare or the community's best interests. The point of view I assumed (which I shall label for the sake of brevity the "primacy of rights") is that in democratic politics, rights and the requirements of justice should have moral primacy. This assumption of the primacy of rights is, as I indicated in Chapter Four, widespread in modern political philosophy.

Communitarians challenge the primacy of rights, for in their view it is based upon a mistaken form of individualism which regards humans as individualized "atomistic" beings who exist prior to society and are unencumbered by a social identity. Since the best-known defenders of the primacy of rights are liberals like John Rawls and Ronald Dworkin, much of the criticism of modern political philosophy by communitarians is directed at liberalism. Individualism has been associated with a wide range of ideas in the history of political thought, and it is impossible to define it in any single, precise way. (Lukes 1973) For communitarians, however, the form of individualism at issue here places such fundamental value on individuals and their rights that it makes insignificant any value that might be placed on community. As MacIntyre provocatively expresses it, "Individualism is and always was the doctrine of successful thieves from the community." (MacIntyre 1976: 181) In other words, a vision of democratic politics that gives primacy to rights is misconceived for communitarians because the form of individualism necessary to ground the primacy of rights is incompatible with the recognition of the moral significance of community. Communitarians offer instead a vision of democratic politics that gives primacy to the promotion and protection of an ideal of the good life that is to be shared in common among individuals. The main idea is that instead of making rights and justice the "first virtue" of social and political institutions, as Rawls urged (Rawls 1971: 3), politics should, to use Charles Taylor's description, "give higher priority to community life or the good of collectivities." (Taylor 1989: 159–160)

The most influential communitarian challenges to the primacy of rights are made by Michael Sandel, Alasdair MacIntyre, and Charles Taylor. There are two especially important lines of criticism of the primacy of rights developed by these philosophers. One line of criticism is designed to show that the very idea of the primacy of rights is incoherent. Taylor and Sandel both explore this line of criticism. The other line of criticism is designed to show that the primacy of rights involves a commitment to an impoverished view of the self. Both Sandel and MacIntyre defend this line of criticism. I shall briefly describe these two lines of criticism in turn.

Consider first the communitarian charge that the idea of the primacy of rights is incoherent. In the two preceding chapters, we discussed respectively entitlement rights to basic liberties and rights to economic equality. The primacy of both types of rights has been questioned by communitarians. For Taylor, the idea that rights to basic liberties should have primacy in accounts of political morality is significant because it means that notions of belonging and duty to one's community are treated as secondary and less important. (Taylor 1985: 188) The reasoning is that the idea that rights to do what you want function as trumps or side-constraints on any limits the community might seek to impose on your freedom. (Taylor 1986: 211) But, for Taylor, careful reflection on the concept of rights reveals a tension. The ascription of rights involves making judgments about which freedoms are valuable and what is worthwhile to do; these sorts of judgments must be made in some sort of moral community with shared values and standards of evaluation. Outside such a community, talk about rights to basic liberties would not be intelligible. Such rights involve, therefore, a certain degree of belonging to a community. How, then, can rights have primacy over the interests of that community? Isn't it inconsistent to insist both on the importance of rights to basic liberties and on giving those rights primacy over the interests of the community in restricting those liberties, since taking them seriously requires also taking the interests of that community seriously?

Michael Sandel points out a similar problem of incoherence in the context of Rawls's difference principle. Recall from the previous chapter that Rawls's difference principle says that social and economic inequalities are justified only when they benefit the worst-off in society. Individuals can be said to have a right to economic equality except when inequalities make them better off. However, as Sandel points out, there is an important sense in which the presumption in favor of equality assumed by Rawls (and most other modern political philosophers) presupposes the fundamental importance of a constitutive community that shares a common good. (Sandel 1982: 79–81) Why else would we think that all individuals should share equally in the economic wealth of the society? As Sandel puts it, "We cannot be persons for whom justice is primary and also be persons for whom the difference principle is a principle of justice." (Sandel 1982: 178) Therefore, it seems incoherent to insist on the primacy of the rights to economic equality of individuals over the interests of the community, since it is precisely because of that community that individuals are thought to have such rights.

Turn now to the line of criticism designed to show that the primacy of rights involves a commitment to a mistaken view of the self and personal identity. (For the sake of brevity, I risk oversimplifying this line of communitarian criticism. See, for a more detailed exposition, Kymlicka 1989a: ch. 4) In §2, it was acknowledged that membership in particular communities is fundamental to our personal identity. For Sandel and MacIntyre, this fact is significant because of the implications for what is the good life for each of us. Both maintain that because who we are is a matter of the social roles we inhabit as members of a particular community, this means that what is good for an individual is not a matter of individual choice but is rather a function of the communities to which he or she belongs. MacIntyre claims, for instance, that "what is good for me has to be the good for one who inhabits these roles." (MacIntyre 1981: 205) Sandel emphasizes that what is at stake here is character:

> . . . to have character is to know that I move in a history I neither summon nor command, which carries consequences none the less for my choices and conduct. It draws me closer to some and more distant from others; it makes some aims more appropriate, others less so. As a self-

interpreting being, I am able to reflect on my history and in this sense to distance myself from it, but the distance is always precarious and provisional, the point of reflection never finally secured outside the history itself. (Sandel 1982: 179)

A major difficulty both MacIntyre and Sandel have with the primacy of rights is that it appears to rest on a view of the self and personal identity that is inconsistent with their view. They believe that the primacy of rights presupposes that it makes sense to talk about what is good for individuals independent of the particular communities to which they belong and the history they share with others. The underlying reason is that since rights are ascribed to individuals because it is good for those individuals to have them and the primacy of rights means that certain rights have priority over what is good for the community, then the ascription of those rights requires an account of what is good for the individual that is not a function of what is good for the communities to which she or he belongs. The upshot is that you can accept either the primacy of rights or their view of the self and personal identity. Since MacIntyre and Sandel think that their view of the self and personal identity is correct, the rejection of the primacy of rights is the only sensible alternative.

§4   THE IDEAL OF THE DEMOCRATIC COMMUNITY

The predominant response to the communitarian challenge to the primacy of rights and justice among other political philosophers is that communitarians misunderstand why in the democratic vision of politics, rights and justice have primacy. What the communitarians overlook is that rights and the other requirements of justice are given primacy in the democratic vision precisely to protect and promote a particular form of community. This particular form of community can be called the ideal of the democratic community. The character of this community and the reason why the primacy of rights is integral to its protection and promotion can be revealed by examining some of the specific responses to the communitarians.

For some feminists, communitarianism is problematic because of its blanket endorsement of all forms of community. (Okin 1989: ch. 3; Friedman 1989: 277–285) Many traditional forms of community are patriarchal and sexist; they often impose huge unfair burdens on women and are built on the rejection of gender equality. Indeed, the examples most often cited by communitarians—family, church congregation, neighborhood—are paradigmatic examples of such traditional forms of community. Their point is that while community may indeed be of moral value, only some forms of community are valuable.

A similar point is made from a postmodernist perspective by philosophers like Iris Young and Drucilla Cornell. Young questions the value of a community understood as unified, with shared goals and aspirations, and a mutual identification. In her view, such a community will suppress differences among its members and exclude from membership those who do not fit in. (Young 1990a: ch. 8; 1990b: 300) Young defends instead the normative ideal of what she calls "city life,"

> The modern city is without walls; it is not planned and coherent. Dwelling in the city means always having a sense of beyond. . . . City life thus . . . embodies difference as the contrary of the face-to-face ideal expressed by most assertions of community. City life is the "being-together" of strangers. Strangers encounter one another . . . acknowledging their contiguity in living. . . . In such encountering people are not "internally" related. . . . They are externally related, they experience each other as other, different, from different groups, histories, professions, cultures, which they do not understand. (Young 1990b: 318)

For her, city life is distinctive because of the requirement of difference and its accommodation of a vast array of "smaller" communities. (Young 1990a: 237)

Cornell too shares reservations about the stifling effect of traditional communities and their antagonism towards difference. Her alternative ideal is not city life but rather what she calls the imaginary domain. (Cornell 1995: ch. 1) The imaginary domain is something we all share, but it is not something concrete, spatial, and material. Instead, it is the rights and the other requirements of social justice that fill the imaginary domain, and the community these requirements foster is in people's thoughts and limited only by their imagination.

Perhaps the strongest response to the communitarian critique of the primacy of rights has come from liberals. Many liberals have argued that communitarians misunderstand the concept of the self required by an intelligible theory of rights. Such a self is not an atomistic being unencumbered by social attachments and commitments. Instead, what is significant is that individuals can revise and adjust their commitments and what they most value in their lives; rights presuppose this capacity for revision and change, rather than a being who has no commitments or sense of value in a community. (Pogge 1989: ch. 2; Kymlicka 1989a: ch. 4; Buchanan 1989: 867–871; Gauthier 1986: ch. 11; Moore 1993: 183–188) This view of the self is modern and certainly controversial, but it is doubtful that much of the communitarian critique applies to it.

Other liberals, most notably John Rawls, have responded to communitarians by insisting that the primacy they accord rights and other requirements of justice does not depend on any sort of controversial idea of the self at all. Rawls maintains that his theory of justice as fairness requires only a political theory of the person. Such a person is "someone who can be a citizen, that is, a normal and fully cooperating member of society over a complete life . . . someone who can take part in, or who can play a role in, social life, and hence exercise and respect its various rights and duties." (Rawls 1993: 18) Moreover, since Rawls situates his theory of justice in the context of a democratic society, citizens are also assumed to be free and equal. (Rawls 1993: 18–20; 1985: 240–244) Rawls's point here is that his assumption of free and equal citizenship is controversial only if you reject the more basic commitment to democracy.

Liberals have also argued that a mistake communitarians make is assuming that rights are necessarily individualistic. There is nothing inherent about the concept of rights that makes it inconceivable to talk about the rights of communities or collective rights. (Kymlicka 1989a: ch 7; Freeden 1990; 1991: ch. 5; Jacobs 1991) Rights exist to protect and promote things that are valuable. Hence, if community is valuable, it may well be sensible to use rights to protect it. Indeed, many liberal philosophers prior to World War II such as L. T. Hobhouse and J. A. Hobson used the language of rights in precisely this way.

Others have also argued that communitarians underestimate the degree to which individual rights actually function to protect even traditional communities. (Raz 1986: 250–255; Buchanan 1989: 858–865) As an illustration, consider the example of an individual's right to freedom of religion. Communitarians characteristically have emphasized how this has enabled individuals to adopt quirky new-age religions or has contributed to secularization and the spread of atheism. However, this right has also enabled traditional religious groups like the Amish to maintain their way of life. Furthermore, there is a sense in which the very idea of a right to freedom of religion depends on the assumption of community. Religious worship seems to have an inherent communal aspect. Does it really make sense to describe a type of behavior as religious if it is only practiced by one individual? The logic of the right to freedom of religion is precisely that it protects particular religious sects and groups by protecting each of its members individually. A similar point can be made about other familiar individual rights such as the right to live one's life free from racial discrimination. This right protects minority racial groups by affording protection to each and everyone of its individual members.

Underlying all of these various—feminist, postmodern, liberal—responses to the communitarian critique of the primacy of rights is the theme that the primacy of rights is not a threat to the value of community but rather is designed to promote a particular form of community as valuable. This particular form is the ideal of democratic community. Democratic community is characterized by significant differences in the personal identity of its members and what they value in their own personal lives. They do not share common aspirations or goals, nor do they share the same religious commitments or sexual orientation, nor are they all of the same racial or ethnic origin. Yet, there is still a bond of community among these individuals. What they share is their common identity as citizens. What distinguishes a democratic community from the sort of political community that is characteristic of aristocracy or a monarchy is that all individuals subject to the government enjoy the status of citizenship; the commitment to political equality distinguishes the modern democratic community from these alternatives.

What is it that ties democratic citizens to each other? The differences in their personal lives and what they value mean that it is impossible to posit some notion of the common good or general welfare. Indeed, we saw in Chapter Two that theories of convergent procedural democracy are all flawed because they require such a notion. What democratic citizens all share is a commitment to the value of democracy as a fair procedure for making collective decisions about matters that affect all of their lives or are necessary for regulating interactions between citizens. Each accepts that despite the disagreements among them, it is of the absolute importance to have regulative political principles. (See, for example, Macedo 1990: ch. 6) This may seem like a superficial sense of community in comparison to the strong ties between people who, say, belong to the same church congregation or are from the same family. But recall also the argument in Chapter Three that the authority of the democratic state rests on its ability to respect the requirements of social justice. It follows that democratic citizens also are linked in their shared commitment to social justice. As Rawls has recently put it, "As citizens they cooperate to achieve their common shared end of justice." (Rawls 1993: 42n) What ties citizens of a democratic community together, then, is their mutual respect for each other. I have tried to emphasize in the preceding chapters that although democratic citizens are likely to disagree about the exact requirements of social justice, especially with regard to when economic and social inequalities are justified, there is still a surprising amount of consensus around the concept of social justice.

When the ideal of the democratic community is described in terms of citizens sharing a commitment to fair democratic procedures and fulfilling the requirements of social justice, the logic of giving rights primacy in the democratic vision of politics seems obvious. In Chapter Four, two types of rights were distinguished; democratic rights, which are those rights that function to ensure fair procedural democracy, and entitlement rights, which identify an individual's fair share of the benefits and burdens of social life. The ideal of a democratic community identifies democratic rights and entitlement rights as the bond shared by its members. Hence, in protecting and promoting that ideal community, those rights should be given primacy. It is important to recall, however, from our discussion of constitutional rights in §6 of Chapter Four that giving rights moral primacy does not necessarily mean that those rights should be constitutionally guaranteed and hence function as trumps on the legislature in a democracy. (See, however, Lund 1990.)

The primacy of rights in the promotion of the ideal of democratic community is reinforced by an insightful observation made by the nineteenth-century intellectual Alexis de Tocqueville in his classic commentary, *Democracy in America*. Tocqueville emphasized that in a democratic community characterized by individuals with very different religious convictions, family values, race and ethnicity, and so on, there is an inherent danger that the binding force of citizenship will disintegrate because people will be constantly drawn into their different private communities and lose a sense of the significance of their identification with others with whom one shares only common citizenship. Although Tocqueville does not endorse this view, it seems sensible to give democratic rights and entitlement rights primacy in order to meet this danger, since an important consequence of giving rights primacy is that the citizenship shared by all individuals, whatever their deep differences in other respects, is too far-reaching and powerful to ignore.

§5   THE PROBLEM OF VULNERABLE MINORITY CULTURES

It has just been explained why the communitarians are mistaken to think that affording moral primacy to individual rights and the other requirements of justice is antagonistic to community. The argument has been made that the primacy of rights protects and promotes the ideal of the democratic community. An important corollary question to ask is whether it is permissible or required of a democratic state ever to promote any forms of community other than the ideal of the democratic community. Is it, for example, permissible for a democratic state to promote a particular religious community? Can a democratic state fund certain artistic communities, such as opera or theater, but not fund baseball or bowling?

Many influential modern political philosophers have defended at some point the general principle of state neutrality as a response to these kinds of questions. (Dworkin 1985: chs. 8, 11; Kymlicka 1989b; Rawls 1993: ch. v) The principle of state neutrality can be understood to require "that the state should not reward or penalize particular conceptions of the good life but, rather, should provide a neutral framework within which different and potentially conflicting conceptions of the good can be pursued." (Kymlicka 1989b: 883) This statement means that the state should be neutral between religions and on the question of whether opera is a better type of leisure time than baseball. Although some of the arguments for state neutrality are complex, the most common argument is quite simple. It says that any alternative to state neutrality would have the effect of not treating everyone fairly, since that would involve the state's promoting some people's interests and not others.

State neutrality has been viewed with considerable skepticism by many modern political philosophers. One line of criticism has been directed at the feasibility of state neutrality. Doubts have been raised about whether it is possible for the state to be neutral consistently. In Stephen Macedo's apt metaphor, state neutrality is a mirage: "The closer we get, the faster the mirage of neutrality vanishes . . . any neutrality . . . is selective, and selective neutrality is not very neutral." (Macedo 1990: 262) The selective character of neutrality is said to be inevitable because it seems impossible to be neutral about the value of neutrality.

The other line of criticism of state neutrality argues that, even if neutrality is feasible, it is not always desirable. (See, for example, Raz 1986: chs. 5–6; Galston 1991: chs. 4–5) The argument here is that sometimes the democratic state should promote certain ways of life and discourage others. The most common rationale is that the democratic state has an interest in their citizens having a particular sort of moral character, a character with moral virtues that sustain a commitment to democratic politics and respect for the rights of others. The state should not, then, be neutral about conceptions of the good and moral character; it should instead promote these particular moral virtues.

If we put aside state neutrality, the important question to be answered is which forms of community should the democratic state seek to create or maintain? One compelling answer is that the state at a minimum has an obligation to maintain the culture of particular vulnerable minority communities in a democracy. This view has been defended at length by Will Kymlicka, who endorses the view defended earlier in §2 that community is significant because of its importance to our sense of who we are. (Kymlicka 1989a; 1995a; 1995b) As he expresses it, "communal and cultural aspects of social life provide the possibility for, and locus of, the pursuit of human values." (Kymlicka 1989a: 253) For individuals, membership in particular communities and cultures is a valuable resource. However, for some individuals, this membership is insecure because the cultural community to which they belong constitutes a small minority in the broader democratic community and is vulnerable for this reason to domination by and assimilation into the larger cultural community. The main example Kymlicka uses is the situation of aboriginal peoples in North America. It is well known that traditional native Indian cultural communities are under threat in our society and have experienced significant disintegration over the past one hundred years. In comparison to members of larger cultural communities in North America, individuals who belong to these aboriginal communities experience a significant unfair disadvantage because of their insecure cultural membership. (Kymlicka 1989a: 190) It follows, according to Kymlicka, that in a democracy committed to fairness, the state should intervene in particular ways that will protect and promote aboriginal communities so that those individuals who belong to these communities will not suffer the disadvantage of insecure membership. In other words, these communities should enjoy a special status in a democracy because of their vulnerability.

There are, however, some serious difficulties with insisting on giving special status to certain vulnerable communities. Do we give this special status to all such communities no matter how small they are or the historical circumstances that caused their vulnerability? (Danley 1991: 181–185) If so, doesn't this end up trivializing the special status, since so many communities would enjoy it? If not, why not, since even the members of the smallest vulnerable communities suffer the disadvantage of insecure membership? Should vulnerable communities be accorded special status when they embody fundamentally undemocratic values such as denying, as some traditional aboriginal cultures do, equal status to men and women? (Moore 1993: 153–155) How should we adjudicate the conflicting claims of two vulnerable cultural communities? How, for example, do we meet the aspirations of francophones in Québec to separate from Canada in order to protect their culture, while meeting the demands of Indians in Québec that they remain in Canada in order to protect theirs?

§6   REVOLUTION, SECESSION, AND CIVIL DISOBEDIENCE

Chapter Three argued that the most compelling explanation for why individuals have an obligation to obey the law of a democratic state appeals to some sort of natural duty to justice. The point is that a democratic state has a special right to rule on the condition that it fulfill the requirements of social justice. Provided that the democratic state does fulfill these requirements, an individual would have an obligation to obey its laws. What should the individual do, though, if the democratic state fails to meet the requirements of social justice?

Presumably, it is important to distinguish among three types of cases. In one case, the democratic state's failure to meet the requirements of social justice is widespread. It might, for example, violate the rights to basic liberties of numerous individuals in a persistent and ongoing manner. What should be done? *Revolution* is the standard response since John Locke to this sort of scenario. Underlying this response is the view that political obligation is based on the state's meeting certain terms including the nonviolation of individual rights. When the state fails to meet these terms, the state ceases to have the authority to rule, and political obligation for the individual dissolves. The revolutionary overthrow of the government by the people is, then, justified. The American Revolution is typically justified in this way.

The second scenario occurs when the injustice is not widespread but is experienced mainly by only one minority group within the society. This was the case, for example, with Roman Catholics in Northern Ireland during the 1960s and with blacks in the state of Mississippi under the Jim Crow laws. One ideal reaction would be for the majority to recognize the injustice and correct it. This is how the civil rights movement in the 1960s is often portrayed. Another possible reaction may be for the minority group to exercise a right to secede. *Secession* would mean that the group would leave the existing democratic community and form instead its own democratic state. An important justification for the right to secede is precisely this sort of group discrimination. (Buchanan 1991: 38–45) By seceding, the group escapes this discrimination.

The third case occurs when the democratic state fails to meet some of the requirements of justice but nonetheless generally does meet the requirements of justice. Neither revolution nor secession seem appropriate. Instead, this seems to be a case for *civil disobedience*. Rawls defines civil disobedience as "a public, nonviolent, conscientious yet political act contrary to law usually done with the aim of bringing about a change in the law or policies of the government." (Rawls 1971: 364) Sit-ins and other forms of illegal demonstrations are standard examples of civil disobedience. What acts of civil disobedience do is to declare that some law or policy is perceived to be contrary to the requirements of justice. If people are assumed to have a natural duty to justice in the sense explained in §3.3 of Chapter Three, then it would follow that people have a derived duty to partake in civil disobedience if the opportunity arises.

What is noteworthy about revolution, secession, and civil disobedience as reactions to a democratic state's not meeting the requirements of social justice is the respect in which all of them require collective action. Revolution and secession obviously involve individuals acting together as a community with a common end. Civil disobedience is more often portrayed as individuals acting on their own, each motivated by her or his own sense of justice and moral outrage. However, like revolution and secession, effective civil disobedience must be coordinated among individuals in a manner that is indicative of a community with a shared sense of purpose. If civil disobedience is indeed an important part of the democratic vision of politics, then such a community would appear to be fundamental. Ironically, the state would seem now to have a good reason to protect and promote a community that exists to express dissent and criticisms of the law and policies of that state.

§7   CONCLUSION

In this final chapter, we have examined the value of community in the democratic vision of politics. The communitarian challenge to the moral primacy of rights is insightful but ultimately fails to undermine the importance modern political philosophers place on rights. The primacy of rights makes sense because of the ideal of the democratic community. That ideal community embraces individuals with a diversity of values and personal commitments who are bound together because of their mutual respect for each other. The question for the democratic state is which other forms of community, if any, should it protect and promote? The promotion of at least two forms of community might make sense in the framework of the democratic vision of politics, although neither is unproblematic. One sort is the vulnerable cultural communities of small minority groups like aboriginal peoples. The other is the community of dissent that is integral to the success of civil disobedience.

SUGGESTED READINGS

1. Sandel, Michael, *Liberalism and the Limits of Justice* (New York, Cambridge University Press, 1982). Probably the most influential statement of the communitarian critique of liberalism, especially Rawls's *A Theory of Justice*.

2. MacIntyre, Alasdair, *After Virtue, Second Edition* (Notre Dame, University of Notre Dame Press, 1985). A provocative critique of most modern moral and political theory.

3. Kymlicka, Will, *Liberalism, Community, and Culture* (New York, Oxford University Press, 1989). A sustained response to the communitarians and a defense of the special rights of minority cultural communities.

4. Okin, Susan Moller, *Justice, Gender, and the Family* (New York, Basic Books,1989). An accessible and careful feminist response to recent philosophical work on social justice, including the communitarians.

5. Kymlicka, Will, editor, *The Rights of Minority Cultures* (New York, Oxford University Press, 1995). A useful collection of many of the best recent philosophical articles on minority cultures and their rights.

References Cited

———————————◆———————————

ABRAHAM, HENRY (1967). *Freedom and the Court: Civil Rights and Liberties in the United States*. New York, Oxford University Press.

ACKERMAN, BRUCE (1980). *Social Justice in the Liberal State*. New Haven, Yale University Press.

ARTHUR, JOHN (1995). *Words That Bind: Judicial Review and the Grounds of Modern Constitutional Theory*. Boulder, CO, Westview Press.

BAILYN, BERNARD (1967). *The Ideological Origins of the American Revolution*. Cambridge, MA, Harvard University Press.

Baker, John (1987). *Arguing for Equality*. New York, Verso Books.

BARBER, BENJAMIN (1984). *Strong Democracy*. Berkeley, CA, University of California Press.

BARRY, BRIAN (1989). *Theories of Justice*. Berkeley, CA, University of California Press.

BARRY, BRIAN (1990). *Political Argument, Reissue*. Berkeley, CA, University of California Press.

BECKER, CARL (1941). *Modern Democracy*. New Haven, CT, Yale University Press.

BEITZ, CHARLES (1989). *Political Equality: An Essay in Democratic Theory*. Princeton, Princeton University Press.

BELL, DANIEL (1993). *Communitarianism and Its Critics*. New York, Oxford University Press.

BELLAH, ROBERT et al. (1985). *Habits of the Heart: Individualism and Commitment in American Life*. New York, Harper & Row.

BERLIN, ISAIAH (1969). *Four Essays on Liberty*. New York, Oxford University Press.

BERLIN, ISAIAH (1980). *Concepts and Categories*. New York, Oxford University Press.

BORK, ROBERT (1990). *The Tempting of America: The Political Seduction of the Law.* New York, Simon & Schuster.

BUCHANAN, ALLEN (1989). "Assessing the Communitarian Critique of Liberalism," *Ethics, vol. 99.*

BUCHANAN, ALLEN (1991). *Secession: The Morality of Political Divorce from Fort Sumter to Lithuania and Quebec.* Boulder, CO, Westview Press.

BUCHANAN, JAMES, and TULLOCK, GORDON (1962). *The Calculus of Consent.* Ann Arbor, MI, University of Michigan Press.

COHEN, G. A. (1981). "Illusions about Freedom and Private Property" in J. Mephan and D. Hillel-Ruben, editors, *Issues in Marxist Philosophy, vol. ix.* Brighton, England, Harvester Press.

COHEN, G. A. (1989). "On the Currency of Egalitarian Justice," *Ethics, vol. 99.*

COHEN, G. A. (1991). "Robert Nozick and Wilt Chamberlain: How Patterns Preserve Liberty" in John Arthur and William Shaw, editors, *Justice and Economic Distribution, Second Edition.* Englewood Cliffs, NJ, Prentice-Hall.

COHEN, G. A. (1992). "Incentives, Inequality, and Community," *The Tanner Lectures on Human Values, vol. 13.* New York, Cambridge University Press.

COLE, G. D. H. (1975). "What Is Socialism?" Reprinted in Anthony De Crespigny and Jeremy Cronin, editors, *Ideologies of Politics.* New York, Oxford University Press.

CONNOLLY, WILLIAM (1983). *The Terms of Political Discourse, Second Edition.* Lexington, MA, D.C. Heath.

CORNELL, DRUCILLA (1995). *The Imaginary Domain.* New York, Routledge.

CROSLAND, C. A. R. (1957). *The Future of Socialism.* New York, MacMillan.

DAHL, ROBERT (1985). *A Preface to Economic Democracy.* Berkeley, CA, University of California Press.

DAHL, ROBERT (1989). *Democracy and Its Critics.* New Haven, CT, Yale University Press.

DANIELS, NORMAN (1975). "Equal Liberty and Unequal Worth of Liberty." Reprinted in Norman Daniels, editor, *Reading Rawls.* Palo Alto, CA, Stanford University Press.

DANIELS, NORMAN, editor (1989). *Reading Rawls, Revised Edition.* Palo Alto, CA, Stanford University Press.

DANLEY, JOHN (1991). "Liberalism, Aboriginal Rights, and Cultural Minorities," *Philosophy & Public Affairs, vol. 20.*

DELUE, STEPHEN (1989). *Political Obligation in a Liberal State.* Albany, State University of New York Press.

DEVLIN, PATRICK (1965). *The Enforcement of Morals.* London, Oxford University Press.

DOWNS, ANTHONY (1957). *An Economic Theory of Democracy.* New York, Harper and Brothers.

DWORKIN, GERALD (1989). *The Theory and Practice of Autonomy.* New York, Cambridge University Press.

DWORKIN, RONALD (1978). *Taking Rights Seriously, New Impression.* Cambridge, MA, Harvard University Press.

DWORKIN, RONALD (1981). "What Is Equality?, Part 2: Equality of Resources," *Philosophy & Public Affairs 10.*

DWORKIN, RONALD (1983). "What Liberalism Isn't," *New York Review of Books,* January 20, 1983.

DWORKIN, RONALD (1985). *A Matter of Principle.* Cambridge, MA, Harvard University Press.

DWORKIN, RONALD (1986). *Law's Empire.* Cambridge, MA, Harvard University Press.

DWORKIN, RONALD (1987). "What Is Equality? Part III: The Place of Liberty," *Iowa Law Review, vol. 72.*

DWORKIN, RONALD (1988). "What Is Equality? Part IV: Political Equality," *University of San Francisco Law Review, vol. 22.*

DWORKIN, RONALD (1990). "Equality, Democracy, and Constitution: We the People in Court," *Alberta Law Review, vol. 28.*

DWORKIN, RONALD (1991). "Liberty and Pornography," *New York Review of Books,* August 15, 1991.

ELSTER, JON (1985). *Making Sense of Marx.* New York, Cambridge University Press.

ELY, JOHN (1980). *Democracy and Distrust.* Cambridge, MA, Harvard University Press.

FEINBERG, JOEL (1973). *Social Philosophy.* Englewood Cliffs, NJ, Prentice-Hall.

FINNIS, JOHN (1980). *Natural Law and Natural Rights.* Oxford, Oxford University Press.

FRANKFURT, Harry (1989). *The Importance of What We Care About.* New York, Cambridge University Press.

FRASER, NANCY (1989). "Talking about Needs: Interpretive Contests as Political Conflicts in Welfare-State Societies," *Ethics, vol. 99.*

FREEDEN, MICHAEL (1990). "Human Rights and Welfare: A Communitarian View," *Ethics, vol. 100.*

FREEDEN, MICHAEL (1991). *"Rights."* Minneapolis, University of Minnesota Press.

FRIED, BARBARA (1995). "Wilt Chamberlain Revisited: Nozick's 'Justice in Transfer' and the Problem of Market-Based Distribution," *Philosophy & Public Affairs, vol. 24.*

FRIEDMAN, MARILYN (1989). "Feminism and Modern Friendship: Dislocating the Community," *Ethics, vol. 99.*

GALLIE, W. B. (1956). "Essentially Contested Concepts," *Proceedings of the Aristotelian Society, vol. 56.*

GALSTON, WILLIAM (1991). *Liberal Purposes: Goods, Virtues, and Diversity in the Liberal State.* New York, Cambridge University Press.

GAUTHIER, DAVID (1996). *Morals by Agreement.* New York, Oxford University Press.

GERAS, NORMAN (1989). "The Controversy about Marx and Justice." Reprinted in Alex Callinicos, editor, *Marxist Theory.* New York, Oxford University Press.

GILLIGAN, CAROL (1982). *In a Different Voice.* Cambridge, MA, Harvard University Press.

GLAZER, NATHAN (1988). *The Limits of Social Policy.* Cambridge, MA, Harvard University Press.

GOODIN, ROBERT (1989), "The State as a Moral Agent" in *The Good Polity,* eds. Alan Hamlin and Philip Pettit. Oxford, Blackwells.

GRAY, JOHN (1978). "On Liberty, Liberalism, and Essential Contestability," *British Journal of Political Science 8.*

GRAY, JOHN (1983). *Mill on Liberty: A Defence.* London, Routledge and Kegan Paul.

GRAY, JOHN (1986). *Liberalism.* Minneapolis: University of Minnesota Press.

GRAY, JOHN, AND PELCZYNSKI, ZBIGNIEW, editors (1984). *Conceptions of Liberty in Political Philosophy.* London, Athlone.

GREEN, LESLIE (1988). *The Authority of the State.* New York, Oxford University Press.

GUTMANN, AMY (1985). "Communitarian Critics of Liberalism," *Philosophy & Public Affairs, vol. 14.*

HART, H. L. A. (1958). "Legal and Moral Obligation." In *Essays in Moral Philosophy.* A. I. Melden, editor. Seattle, University of Washington Press.

HART, H. L. A. (1961). *The Concept of Law.* Oxford, Oxford University Press.

HART, H. L. A. (1963). *Law, Liberty, and Morality.* Palo Alto: CA, Stanford University Press.

HART, H. L. A. (1982). *Essays on Bentham.* Oxford, Oxford University Press.

HART, H. L. A. (1983) *Essays on Jurisprudence and Philosophy.* Oxford, Oxford University Press.

HART, H. L. A. (1984). "Are There Any Natural Rights?" In *Theories of Rights.* Jeremy Waldron, editor. New York, Oxford University Press.

HARTMANN, HEIDI (1981). "The Unhappy Marriage of Marxism and Feminism." Reprinted in Lydia Sargent, editor, *The Unhappy Marriage of Marxism and Feminism.* London, Pluto Press.

HAYEK, FREDERICK (1960). *The Constitution of Liberty.* Chicago, University of Chicago Press.

HAYEK, FREDERICK (1982). *Law, Liberty, and Legislation, Vol. II: The Mirage of Social Justice.* London, Routledge and Kegan Paul.

HELD, DAVID (1987). *Models of Democracy.* Palo Alto, CA, Stanford University Press.

HOLMES, STEPHEN (1989). "The Permanent Structure of Antiliberal Thought." In Nancy Rosenblum, editor, *Liberalism and the Moral Life.* Cambridge, MA, Harvard University Press.

HUME, DAVID (1748). "Of the Original Contract." In *Social Contract.* Ernest Barker, editor. Oxford, Oxford University Press, 1960.

ITZIN, CATHERINE, editor (1992). *Pornography: Women, Violence, and Civil Liberties.* New York, Oxford University Press.

JACOBS, LESLEY (1991). "Bridging the Gap Between Individual and Collective Rights with the Idea of Integrity," *The Canadian Journal of Law & Jurisprudence, vol. iv.*

JACOBS, LESLEY (1993a). *Rights and Deprivation.* New York, Oxford University Press.

JACOBS, LESLEY (1993b) "Realizing Equal Life Prospects" in *New Approaches to Welfare Theory*, Glenn Drover and Pat Kerans, editors. London, Edward Algar.

JACOBS, LESLEY (1993c). "The Enabling Model of Rights," *Political Studies, vol. 41.*

JACOBS, LESLEY (1994). "Equal Opportunity and Gender Disadvantage," *The Canadian Journal of Law and Jurisprudence, vol. VII.*

JACOBSON, DANIEL (1995). "Freedom of Speech Acts? A Response to Langton," *Philosophy & Public Affairs 24.*

JONES, PETER (1983). "Political Equality and Majority Rule," in David Miller and Larry Siedentop, editors, *The Nature of Political Theory*. New York, Oxford University Press.

KATEB, GEORGE (1989). "Liberal Individuality and the Meaning of Rights" in Nancy Rosenblum, editor, *Liberalism and the Moral Life*. Cambridge, MA, Harvard University Press.

KAUS, MICKEY (1992). *The End of Equality*. New York, Basic Books.

KELMAN, STEVEN (1987). *Making Public Policy*, New York, Basic Books.

KLOSKO, GEORGE (1992). *The Principle of Fairness and Political Obligation*. Lanham, MD, Rowman and Littlefield.

KLOSKO, GEORGE (1994). "Political Obligation and the Natural Duties of Justice," *Philosophy & Public Affairs, vol. 23.*

KRISTOL, IRVING (1971). "Pornogaphy, Obscenity, and the Case for Censorship." Reprinted in Joel Feinberg and Hyman Gross, editors, *Philosophy of Law, Fourth Edition*. Belmont, CA, Wadsworth Publishers.

KYMLICKA, WILL (1988). "Liberalism and Communitarianism," *Canadian Journal of Philosophy, vol. 18.*

KYMLICKA, WILL (1989a). *Liberalism, Community, and Culture*. New York, Oxford University Press.

KYMLICKA, WILL (1989b). "Liberal Individualism and Liberal Neutrality," *Ethics, vol. 99.*

KYMLICKA, WILL (1990). *Contemporary Political Philosophy*. New York, Oxford University Press.

KYMLICKA, WILL (1995a). *Multicultural Citizenship: A Liberal Theory of Minority Rights*. New York, Oxford University Press.

KYMLICKA, WILL, editor (1995b). *The Rights of Minority Cultures*. New York, Oxford University Press.

LANGTON, RAE (1993). "Speech Acts and Unspeakable Acts," *Philosophy & Public Affairs 22.*

LARABEE, MARY JEANNE, editor (1993). *An Ethic of Care*. New York, Routledge.

LIPSON, LESLIE (1964). *The Democratic Civilization*. New York, Oxford University Press.

LUKES, STEVEN (1973). *Individualism*. Cambridge, MA, Basil Blackwell.

LUND, WILLIAM (1990). "Communitarian Politics, the Supreme Court, and Privacy: The Continuing Need for Liberal Boundaries," *Social Theory and Practice, vol. 16.*

LYONS, DAVID, editor (1979). *Rights*. Belmont, CA, Wadsworth.

MacCallum, Gerald (1972). "Negative and Positive Freedom," reprinted in Peter Laslett, editor, *Philosophy, Politics, and Society, Fourth Series*. New York, Cambridge University Press.

MacCormick, Neil (1978). "Rights in Legislation" in P. M. S. Hacker and J. Raz, editors, *Law, Morality, and Society*. Oxford, Oxford University Press.

Macedo, Stephen (1990). *Liberal Virtues: Citizenship, Virtue, and Community in Liberal Constitutionalism*. New York, Oxford University Press.

MacIntyre, Alasdair (1976). "On Democratic Theory," *Canadian Journal of Philosophy, vol. VI*.

MacIntyre, Alasdair (1981). *After Virtue*. Notre Dame, University of Notre Dame Press.

MacKinnon, Catharine (1987). *Feminism Unmodified*. Cambridge, MA, Harvard University Press.

MacKinnon, Catharine (1989). *Toward a Feminist Theory of the State*. Cambridge, MA, Harvard University Press.

MacKinnon, Catharine (1994). *Only Words, Revised Edition*. London, Harper Collins.

Macpherson, C. B. (1977). *The Life and Times of Liberal Democracy*. New York, Oxford University Press.

Mansbridge, Jane (1986). *Why We Lost the ERA*. Chicago, IL, University of Chicago Press.

Marshall, T. H. (1950). *Citizenship and Social Class and other essays*. Cambridge, England, Cambridge University Press.

McLean, Iain. (1989). *Democracy and New Technology*. Palo Alto, CA, Stanford University Press.

Mill, John Stuart (1859). *On Liberty and other essays*, John Gray, editor. New York, Oxford University Press, 1991.

Miller, David (1989). *Market, State, and Community: Theoretical Foundations of Market Socialism*. Oxford, Oxford University Press.

Miller, David, editor (1991). *Liberty*. New York, Oxford University Press.

Minnow, Martha (1990). *Making All the Difference*. Ithaca, NY, Cornell University Press.

Minnow, Martha, and Shanley, Mary (1996). "Relational Rights and Responsibility," *Hypathia, vol 11(1)*.

Moore, Margaret (1993). *Foundations of Liberalism*. New York, Oxford University Press.

Mulhall, Stephen, and Swift, Adam (1992). *Liberals and Communitarians*. Cambridge, MA, Basil Blackwell.

Murphy, Mark (1994). "Acceptance of Authority and the Duty to Comply with Just Institutions: A Comment on Waldron," *Philosophy & Public Affairs, vol. 23*.

Murray, Charles (1984). *Losing Ground: American Solicy Policy from 1950 to 1980*. New York, Basic Books.

Myrdal, Gunnar (1944). *An American Dilemma: The Negro Problem and Modern Democracy*. New York, Harper and Brothers.

NAGEL, THOMAS (1982). "Libertarianism Without Foundations" in Jeffrey Paul, editor, *Reading Nozick*. Cambridge, MA, Basil Blackwell.

NELSON, WILLIAM (1980). *On Justifying Democracy*. London, Routledge and Kegan Paul.

NOZICK, ROBERT (1974). *Anarchy, State, and Utopia*. New York, Basic Books.

OAKESHOTT, MICHAEL (1962). *Rationalism in Politics and other essays*. London, Methuen.

OKIN, SUSAN MOLLER (1987). "Justice and Gender," *Philosophy & Public Affairs, vol. 16*.

OKIN, SUSAN MOLLER (1989). *Justice, Gender, and the Family*. New York, Basic Books.

OKIN, SUSAN MOLLER (1991). "Economic Equality After Divorce," *Dissent* (Summer 1991), 383–385.

PATEMAN, CAROLE (1989). *The Disorder of Women: Democracy, Feminism, and Political Theory*. Palo Alto, CA, Stanford University Press.

PAUL, JEFFREY (1984). "Rawls on Liberty" in John Gray and Zbigniew Pelczynski, editors, *Conceptions of Liberty in Political Philosophy*. London, Athlone Press.

PEFFER, RODNEY (1990). *Marx, Morality, and Social Justice*. Princeton, NJ, Princeton University Press.

PHILLIPS, Anne (1991). *Engendering Democracy*. University Park, Pennsylvania State University Press.

PHILLIPS, DEREK (1993). *Looking Backward: A Critical Appraisal of Communitarian Thought*. Princeton, NJ, Princeton University Press.

PLAMENATZ, JOHN (1962). *Man and Society, Volume One*. London, Longmans.

POCOCK, J. G. A. (1975). *The Machiavellian Moment*. New York, Cambridge University Press.

POGGE, THOMAS (1989). *Realizing Rawls*. Ithaca, NY, Cornell University Press.

PRZEWORSKI, ADAM (1987), "Democracy as a Contingent Outcome of Conflicts." In *Constitutionalism and Democracy*. Jon Elster and Rune Slagstad, editors. New York, Cambridge University Press.

PRZEWORSKI, ADAM (1991). *Democracy and the Market*. New York, Cambridge University Press.

RAPHAEL, D. D. (1990). *Problems of Political Philosophy, Second Edition*. London, MacMillan.

RAWLS, JOHN (1958). "Justice as Fairness." Reprinted in Steven M. Cahn and Joram G, Haber, *20th Century Ethical Theory*. Englewood Cliffs, NJ, Prentice-Hall.

RAWLS, JOHN (1971). *A Theory of Justice*. Cambridge, MA, Harvard University Press.

RAWLS, JOHN (1985) "Justice as Fairness, Political, not Metaphysical," *Philosophy and Public Affairs, vol. 14*.

RAWLS, JOHN (1987). "The Idea of an Overlapping Consensus," *Oxford Journal of Legal Studies, vol. 7*.

RAWLS, JOHN (1993). *Political Liberalism*. New York, Columbia University Press.

RAZ, JOSEPH (1986). *The Morality of Freedom*. New York, Oxford University Press.

RHODE, DEBORAH (1989). *Justice and Gender.* Cambridge, MA, Harvard University Press.

ROEMER, JOHN (1992). "The Morality and Efficiency of Market Socialism," *Ethics, vol. 102.*

ROEMER, JOHN (1994). *A Future for Socialism.* New York, Verso Books.

RORTY, RICHARD (1985). "Solidarity or Objectivity" in John Rajchman and Cornell West, editors, *Post-Analytic Philosophy.* New York, Columbia University Press.

RORTY, RICHARD (1989). *Contingency, Irony, and Solidarity.* New York, Cambridge University Press.

ROUSSEAU, JEAN-JACQUES (1762). *The Social Contract.* In *The Essential Rousseau.* Lowell Bair, trans. New York, Mentor Books, 1974.

SANDEL, MICHAEL (1982). *Liberalism and the Limits of Justice.* New York, Cambridge University Press.

SANDEL, MICHAEL (1984). "Morality and the Liberal Ideal." Reprinted in John Arthur and William Shaw, editors, *Justice and Economic Distribution, Second Edition.* Englewood Cliffs, NJ, Prentice-Hall.

SANDEL, MICHAEL (1996a). "America's Search for a New Public Philosophy," *The Atlantic Monthly,* March 1996.

SANDEL, MICHAEL (1996b). *Democracy's Discontent: America's Search for a New Public Philosophy.* Cambridge, MA, Harvard University Press.

SCANLON, T. (1972). "A Theory of Freedom of Expression." Reprinted in R. M. Dworkin, editor, *The Philosophy of Law.* New York, Oxford University Press.

SCANLON, T. (1975). "Rawls's Theory of Justice." Reprinted in Norman Daniels, editor, *Reading Rawls, Second Edition.* Palo Alto, CA, Stanford University Press.

SCANLON, T. (1979). "Freedom of Expression and Categories of Expression," *University of Pittsburgh Law Review 40, 519–550.*

SCHEFFLER, SAMUEL (1982). "Natural Rights, Equality, and the Minimal State" in Jeffrey Paul, editor, *Reading Nozick.* Cambridge, MA, Basil Blackwell.

SCHUMPETER, JOSEPH (1950). *Capitalism, Socialism, and Democracy, 3rd ed.* New York, Harper and Brothers.

SEN, AMARTYA (1992). *Inequality Reexamined.* Cambridge, MA, Harvard University Press.

SIMMONS, A. JOHN (1979). *Moral Principles and Political Obligations.* Princeton, NJ, Princeton University Press.

SKINNER, QUENTIN (1984). "The Idea of Negative Liberty: philosophical and historical perspectives" in Richard Rorty, J. B. Schneewind, and Quentin Skinner, editors, *Philosophy in History.* New York, Cambridge University Press.

SKINNER, QUENTIN (1986). "The Paradoxes of Political Liberty," *The Tanner Lectures on Human Values, vol. VII.*

SOPER, PHILIP (1984). *A Theory of Law.* Cambridge, MA, Harvard University Press.

STEINER, HILLEL (1994). *An Essay on Rights.* Cambridge, MA, Basil Blackwell.

STROSSEN, NADINE (1995). *Defending Pornography: Free Speech, Sex, and the Fight for Women's Rights*. New York, Simon & Schuster.

TAWNEY, R. H. (1964). *Equality*, Fourth Edition. London, Unwin.

TAYLOR, CHARLES (1985). *Philosophy and the Human Sciences, Philosophical Papers 2*. New York, Cambridge University Press.

TAYLOR, CHARLES (1986). "Alternative Futures: Legitimacy, Identity and Alienation in Late-Twentieth Century Canada" in Alan Cairns and Cynthia Williams, editors, *Constitutionalism, Citizenship, and Sociey in Canada*. Toronto, University of Toronto Press.

TAYLOR, CHARLES (1989). "Cross-Purposes: The Liberal-Communitarian Debate" in Nancy Rosenblum, editor, *Liberalism and the Moral Life*. Cambridge, MA, Harvard University Press.

THERNSTROM, ABIGAIL (1987). *Whose Votes Count?: Affirmative Action and Minority Voting Rights*. Cambridge, MA, Harvard University Press.

TOCQUEVILLE, ALEXIS DE (1835). *Democracy in America*. George Lawrence, trans. J. P. Mayer, editor. Garden City, NY, Anchor Books, 1969.

TUCKER, ROBERT, editor (1980). *The Marx-Engels Reader*. New York: Norton and Norton.

UNGER, ROBERTA (1983). *The Critical Legal Studies Movement*. Cambridge, MA, Harvard University Press.

VAN PARIJS, PHILLIPPE (1992). "Basic Income Capitalism," *Ethics, vol. 102*.

VARIAN, HAL (1975). "Distributive Justice, Welfare Economics, and the Theory of Fairness," *Philosophy & Public Affairs 4*.

WALDRON, JEREMY (1982). "The Right to do Wrong," *Ethics 92*.

WALDRON, JEREMY, editor (1984). *Theories of Rights*. New York, Oxford University Press.

WALDRON, JEREMY (1988). *The Right to Private Property*. Oxford, Oxford University Press.

WALDRON, JEREMY (1989). "Autonomy and Perfectionism in Raz's *Morality of Freedom*," *Southern California Law Review, vol. 62*.

WALDRON, JEREMY (1993a). "Special Ties and Natural Duties," *Philosophy & Public Affairs, vol. 22*.

WALDRON, JEREMY (1993b). "A Right-Based Critique of Constitutional Rights," *Oxford Journal of Legal Studies, vol 13*, 18–51.

WALDRON, JEREMY (1993c). *Liberal Rights*. New York, Cambridge University Press.

WALZER, MICHAEL (1983). *Spheres of Justice: A Defense of Pluralism and Equality*. New York, Basic Books.

WALZER, MICHAEL (1990). "The Communitarian Critique of Liberalism," *Political Theory, vol. 18*.

WEITZMAN, LENORE (1986). *The Divorce Revolution: The Unexpected Social and Economic Consequences for Women and Children*. New York, The Free Press.

WOLFF, ROBERT PAUL (1970). *In Defense of Anarchism*. New York, Harper Torchbooks.

WOLFF, ROBERT PAUL (1977). *Understanding Rawls*. Princeton, NJ, Princeton University Press.

WOLIN, SHELDON (1996). "The Liberal/Democratic Divide," *Political Theory 24 (1)*, 97–119.

WOOD, ALLEN (1986). "Marx and Equality." Reprinted in John Roemer, editor, *Analytical Marxism*. New York, Cambridge University Press.

YOUNG, IRIS MARION (1990a). *Justice and the Politics of Difference*. Princeton, NJ, Princeton University Press.

YOUNG, IRIS MARION (1990b). "The Ideal of Community and the Politics of Difference." Reprinted in Linda Nicholson, editor, *Feminism/Postmodernism*. New York, Routledge.

YOUNG, ROBERT (1986). *Personal Autonomy: Beyond Negative and Positive Liberty*. Sydney, Croom Helm.

Index

Tullock, G., 22
tyranny of the majority, 69

W

Waldron, J., 35, 46, 49, 56, 65, 67, 81, 83
Walzer, M., 97, 101, 105
Weitzman, L., 94
welfare-state, 72, 80
Wolff, R., 11, 35, 76
Wolin, S., 65
Wood, A., 97
worth of liberty, 78

U

utilitarianism, 44, 52

V

Van Parijs, P., 98
Varian, H., 22
voting and elections, 6, 18, 22, 23, 32, 39–41, 59–61, 65
vulnerable minorities, 32, 65–66

Y

Young, I., 100, 101, 110
Young, R., 83